Workshop on Future Directions and Needs in the Spoken Dialog Community 2012 (SDCTD 2012)

Tools and Data

Held at the 2012 Conference of the North American Chapter of the Association for Computational Linguistics: Human Language Technologies (NAACL-HLT 2012)

Montreal, Quebec, Canada
3-8 June 2012

ISBN: 978-1-62276-546-1

Printed from e-media with permission by:

Curran Associates, Inc.
57 Morehouse Lane
Red Hook, NY 12571

proceedings.com

Some format issues inherent in the e-media version may also appear in this print version.

Printed by Curran Associates, Inc. (2013)

Association for Computational Linguistics
209 N. Eighth Street
Stroudsburg, Pennsylvania 18360

Phone: 1-570-476-8006
Fax: 1-570-476-0860

acl@aclweb.org

Additional copies of this publication are available from:

Curran Associates, Inc.
57 Morehouse Lane
Red Hook, NY 12571 USA
Phone: 845-758-0400
Fax: 845-758-2634
Email: curran@proceedings.com
Web: www.proceedings.com

Preface

With a large and diverse Spoken Dialog research community that is characterized by its rapid progress and innovation, the SDCTD 2012 workshop is designed to take the pulse of this community, underlining its most advanced discoveries, charting its future directions and tracking its needs. The workshop includes position papers from eminent researchers in the field on a variety of topics that can be grouped under the following five topics:

- Knowledge Acquisition and Resource Creation
- Assessment
- New Technologies for Spoken Dialogue Systems
- Architectures
- Community Building

The spoken dialog research community has interests in specific topics such as belief tracking, multimodal dialog, simulated users, dialog assessment, etc. This diversity of interests makes it difficult to find common threads that can bind the community together. The workshop aims at discovering those common threads. We can cite three types of existing common tools and data. One is data sharing. Another is the Spoken Dialog Challenge, which enables many researchers to compare techniques on a common task. Yet another is the use of a well-documented platform that can be used to teach new researchers about spoken dialog architecture, thus enabling easier entry to our field.

The workshop will have the following structure:
In the morning, speakers will cover the main advances that have been made on each of the five topics in the past five years and then point to specific promising areas of research. We will then have a poster session, reviewing recent projects and tools. In the afternoon, Participants will split into breakout groups on these topics and the groups will report back to all of the participants to attempt to define needs that are common across topics and thus the most widespread in the community. The end of day reports will be available from the workshop website: `http://projects.ict.usc.edu/nld/SDCTD2012/`

Maxine Eskenazi, Alan Black, David Traum, Workshop Chairs

Organizers:

Maxine Eskenazi Carnegie Mellon University
Alan Black Carnegie Mellon University
David Traum USC Institute for Creative Technologies

Program Committee:

Table of Contents

Workshop Program

Thursday, June 7, 2012

Thursday, June 7, 2012 (continued)

Up from Limited Dialog Systems!

Giuseppe Riccardi
University of Trento
via Sommarive, 14
38050, Trento, Italy
riccardi@disi.unitn.it

Philipp Cimiano
Bielefeld University
Universitätsstraße 21–23
33615, Bielefeld, Germany
cimiano@cit-ec.uni-bielefeld.de

Alexandros Potamianos
Technical University of Crete
73100, Chania
Crete, Greece
potam@telecom.tuc.gr

Christina Unger
Bielefeld University
Universitätsstraße 21–23
33615, Bielefeld, Germany
cunger@cit-ec.uni-bielefeld.de

Abstract

In the last two decades, information-seeking spoken dialog systems (SDS) have moved from research prototypes to real-life commercial applications. Still, dialog systems are limited by the scale, complexity of the task and coverage of knowledge required by problem-solving machines or mobile personal assistants. Future spoken interaction are required to be multilingual, understand and act on large scale knowledge bases in all its forms (from structured to unstructured). The Web research community have striven to build large scale and open multilingual resources (e.g. Wikipedia) and knowledge bases (e.g. Yago). We argue that a) it is crucial to leverage this massive amount of Web lightly structured knowledge and b) the scale issue can be addressed collaboratively and design open standards to make tools and resources available to the whole speech and language community.

1 Introduction

In the last two decades, interactive spoken dialog systems (SDS) have moved from research prototypes to real-life commercial applications (Tur and De Mori, 2011). Generally, SDS are built for a specific task (e.g. call routing) with ad-hoc limited knowledge base and for a predefined target language. However, one major limitation in commercial SDS prototyping is that they are not easily and quickly extensible and portable to new domains or languages. Such porting requirements range from defining (or extending) a domain ontology to handcrafting a new grammar or training stochastic models for speech recognition and understanding. These are the research and engineering goals motivating the PortDial project whose objectives include the engagement of the whole technical community. In the PortDial project we would like to engage researchers in building resources that may be generated via top-down processes (grammars), bottom-up processes (statistical models) or via a fusion of both. In this position paper we want to address the critical limitations of SDS systems: a) poor ability to cover the knowledge space and its interface to the SDS components (speech recognition, language understanding and dialog manager) and b) collaboratively design open standards to make tools and resources available to the whole speech and language community.

2 Exploiting top-down knowledge

There are at least three main kinds of structured knowledge sources that SDS modules may exploit: ontologies, grammars, and lexica. *Ontologies* explicitly model background knowledge about a certain domain. In the last years, many free and open collaboratively created resources have emerged, including large multi-lingual corpora such as Wikipedia, and broad-coverage ontologies, e.g. as part of the Linked Data Cloud (Bizer et al., 2009), either created manually or extracted automatically from existing data (such as DBpedia or Yago). However, while also *lexica* such as Wiktionary are available today on the Web, ontologies typically lack information about linguistic realization. For this reason, ontologies available on the Web are not directly exploitable by dialog systems. Linguistic information is commonly captured in *grammars*, that are either hand-crafted or created by means of machine learning techniques. In order to be able to generate high-quality grammars with as little manual effort as possible, we aim at (semi) automating the knowledge-based generation of lexica and grammars. To achieve this, it is crucial to leverage Web resources for enriching ontologies with lexical and linguistic information, i.e. information about how ontological concepts are lexicalized in different languages, capturing in particular lexical and syntactic variation (Unger et al., 2010). This knowledge-centered grammar generation process may be merged with methods for automatically inferring structure from lightly annotated corpus, including data harvested from the Web, in a bottom-up fashion (Tur and De Mori, 2011). For a dialog system to be able to exploit ontologies, lexica and grammars, these three resources need to be tightly aligned, i.e. they need to share domain-relevant vocabulary. For this alignment, we propose to build on Semantic Web standards, mainly in order to support the incorporation of already existing data, to share resources for SDS engineering, and facilitate collaborative knowledge engineering. From a larger perspective, such an approach has the potential of creating SDS resources (ontologies, lexica and grammars) that are strongly aligned with each other as well as with other resources available on the Web, thus fostering the creation of an eco-system of linked resources that can be reused to facilitate the process of engineering and porting a dialog system to new domains and languages.

3 Collaboratively building and sharing knowledge

Today the lack of reusable linguistic resources and annotated data hinders the rapid development of spoken dialog systems in industry and academia alike. Despite progress in standardization of the format of SDS grammars and semantic representations, the data proper has to be hand-crafted for new applications and languages with little or no automation available. We argue above that language engineering technology is now mature to help create such linguistic resources automatically or semi-automatically using data that is either harvested from the web or via community crowdsourcing using the "collective wisdom of expert crowds". Although providing linguistic resources and tools for cost-effective SDS development is important and relevant, a data pool that is not openly sharable and continuously enriched fails its purpose. It is thus important to guarantee the sustainability of the linguistic SDS resources engineered via a community that both uses and actively develops the data pool. Towards this end, we envision both a free and premium data exchange targeting non-commercial users that can maintain and enrich the free version of the data pool, and commercial speech services developers that can contribute to the premium data pool via an electronic marketplace. This is the model we are launching within the EC-funded PortDial project and aiming at involving the research community at large and existing communities for sharing linguistic resources, such as METANET and METASHARE[1]. We believe that the creation of sharable SDS data and linguistic resources for both academic and commercial use will lead to the democratization of spoken dialog systems development, reduce the barrier to entry for new developers, as well as lead to improved technologies for authoring speech services.

References

C. Bizer, T. Heath, and T. Berners-Lee. 2009. Linked data-the story so far. *International Journal on Semantic Web and Information Systems*, 14:9.

G. Tur and R. De Mori, editors. 2011. *Spoken Language Understanding: Systems for Extracting Semantic Information from Speech*. Wiley.

Christina Unger, Felix Hieber, and Philipp Cimiano. 2010. Generating LTAG grammars from a lexicon-ontology interface. In Srinivas Bangalore, Robert Frank, and Maribel Romero, editors, *Proceedings of the 10th International Workshop on Tree Adjoining Grammars and Related Formalisms (TAG+10)*, pages 61–68, 06/2010.

[1] `http://www.meta-net.eu/meta-share`

Directions for Research on Spoken Dialog Systems, Broadly Defined*

Nigel G. Ward
University of Texas at El Paso
El Paso, Texas 79968, USA
nigelward@acm.org

Abstract

To increase impact and accelerate progress, the spoken dialog systems research community should work on four shareable things that will also engage and support sister fields of science and engineering.

1 To Reach Out to the VoiceXML Community, a Commercial-Dialogs Corpus

Although many people are frustrated with the commercial dialog systems they use every day, spoken dialog systems research has been only sporadically relevant to these issues. Although service interactions are pervasive in everyday life, and can be rich and interesting, the vast majority of attempts to model and engineer them have attempted to optimize efficiency and surface-goal completion. The results are all around us, from crudely scripted upselling attempts at fast food restaurants to stilted dialog systems that tediously elicit the pieces of information needed to complete a database query. One reason is that the research community has come to shun most practical dialog types, perhaps to avoid seeming old-fashioned or being tainted by low expectations, or perhaps due to a misperception that industry is addressing these issues. A resource that would help progress here would be a commercial-dialogs corpora that is shareable by all.

Personally, I would like this corpus to be one with a truly exemplary person in the service role, someone who puts customers at ease, develops rapport, brings humor and sparkle, and makes them want to call back. Having several thousand short dialogs where diverse customers call in to that person, and modeling how she handles them, would take us a long way to understanding responsive and adaptive behaviors. Even prototype systems built on such dialogs could help set the agenda for future generations of commercial dialog systems.

*This work was supported by NSF Award IIS-0914868.

2 To Reach Out to the Applied Linguistics Communities, Dialog Analysis Tools

Although many people are fascinated by language and dialog, spoken dialog systems research has only sporadically tapped this enthusiasm. For example, researchers in the conversation analysis tradition and teachers of foreign languages, not to mention many undergraduates, love to explore patterns of dialog. However spoken dialog research so far has produced scant findings about language behavior that are interesting to and graspable by non-engineers.

Personally, I think the biggest opportunity here involves tools to support non-technical people in discovering things themselves. Even amateurs, such as high school science fair participants, should be able to satisfy curiosity or confirm hunches, and experience the joy of systematically examining dialog phenomena. Our community ought to be producing tools and toolsets that support the complete workflow in such inquiries, eclectically supporting tagging, searching, juxtaposing clips and so on, and supporting both perceptually-based analysis and quantitative analysis in an integrated way. In particular we need to go beyond in-lab solutions (Ward and Al Bayyari, 2006) to develop robust toolsets that can be used effectively without months of training.

3 To Reach Out to the Psycholinguistics Community, Modeling-Related Goals

Although many people are curious about how communication feats are achieved daily by human minds, spoken dialog research has only sporadically raised questions of real scientific interest. The spoken dialog community ought to formulate one or two high-profile grand-challenge problems that would inspire and bring people together, either cooperatively or in competition. Rather than "dialog management" and systems-type problems, these should be framed as "dialog modeling" problems, to make it clear that they are true scientific problems, and formulated so that they can be addressed more empirically and/or more theoretically, without requiring researchers to work with end-to-end systems. Such purer formulations should also help focus on questions of the fundamental human perceptions and abilities involved here, and how they vary with age, personality, language and culture.

Personally I think the most central and dialog-specific issues in our field are those relating to interpersonal coordination. Topics here have been nibbled at, perhaps most saliently in the study of turn-taking phenomena. Possible grand challenges may relate to topics such as "dialog dynamics" and "prediction of the interlocutor's actions," but formulating these problems so that they are general, and yet relevant and tractable, has been difficult (Ward, 2010; Ward et al., 2010).

4 To Reach Out to the Speech Processing Community, More Open Models

First, although speech generation and speech synthesis researchers are currently looking for new challenges, beyond correctness and intelligibilty, the dialog systems community has only sporadically offered them interesting goals. These systems need somehow to be able to express the richness of the attitudes, structures, and intentions people convey in dialog, in real time, and we ought to provide specifications for this. Personally I think that multi-dimensional vector-space models of dialog states, situations, and intentions have promise here, and that these can best be developed by bottom-up empirical studies (Ward and Vega, 2012 submitteda), one of which suggests that the important dimensions of dialog include, at least, in rough order of importance: who has the floor, the activity level, topic aging and transition, turn taking, seeking vs. establishing grounding, empathy, and sympathy, lexical access and planning processes, dominance, confidence, affect and attitude, rhetorical structure and strategy, and indications of concentration and involvement.

Second, although research on emotion and other nonverbal aspects of speech is advancing, this has only sporadically been guided by the needs of dialog systems. We ought to be thinking more about how emotion, attitude, stance, and related dimensions of communication are used in dialog. Personally I think that empirical studies of prosody, again, can be informative.

Third, although speech recognition researchers are adding flexibility and incrementality, speech recognizers' interactions with the dialog manager are still very limited. In particular, the role of the dialog model in telling the recognizer what words are likely to come next, that is, its role in language modeling, is still underdeveloped. Personally I think we need dialog models that track more aspects of the dialog, and do so continuously, and supply that information to the recognizer (Ward and Vega, 2012 submittedb).

References

Nigel Ward and Yaffa Al Bayyari. 2006. A case study in the identification of prosodic cues to turn-taking: Back-channeling in Arabic. In *Interspeech 2006 Proceedings*.

Nigel G. Ward and Alejandro Vega. 2012, submitteda. A bottom-up exploration of the dimensions of dialog state in spoken interaction. In *Sigdial*.

Nigel G. Ward and Alejandro Vega. 2012, submittedb. Towards empirical dialog-state modeling and its use in language modeling. In *Interspeech*.

Nigel G. Ward, Olac Fuentes, and Alejandro Vega. 2010. Dialog prediction for a general model of turn-taking. In *Interspeech*.

Nigel G. Ward. 2010. The challenge of modeling dialog dynamics. In *Workshop on Modeling Human Communication Dynamics, at Neural Information Processing Systems*.

Position Paper: Towards Standardized Metrics and Tools for Spoken and Multimodal Dialog System Evaluation

Sebastian Möller, Klaus-Peter Engelbrecht, Florian Kretzschmar, Stefan Schmidt, Benjamin Weiss
Quality and Usability Lab, Telekom Innovation Laboratories, TU Berlin
Ernst-Reuter-Platz 7
10587 Berlin, Germany
sebastian.moeller@telekom.de

Abstract

We argue that standardized metrics and automatic evaluation tools are necessary for speeding up knowledge generation and development processes for dialog systems.

1 Introduction

The Spoken Dialogue Challenge launched by CMU (Black et al., 2011) provides a common platform for dialog researchers in order to test the performance of their systems and components against the state-of-the-art. Still, evaluations are individual undertakings in most areas, as common metrics and procedures which would be applicable for a range of systems are sparse. In the following, it is argued that significant progress can be made if three prerequisites are available:

- Common metrics for quantifying user and system interaction behavior and perceived quality
- Reliable models for predicting user judgments on the basis of automatically-extracted or annotated interaction metrics
- Methods for realistically simulating user behavior in response to dialog systems

The state-of-the-art and necessary research in these three areas is outlined in the following paragraphs. The Spoken Dialogue Challenge can contribute to validating such metrics and models.

2 Common Metrics

Whereas early assessment and evaluation cycles were based on ad-hoc selected metrics, approaches have been made to come up with a standard set of metrics for quantifying interactions between users and systems which would make evaluation exercises comparable. The International Telecommunication Union (ITU-T) has standardized two sets of metrics: ITU-T Suppl. 24 to P-Series (2005) for spoken dialog systems, and ITU-T Suppl. 25 to P-Series Rec. (2011) for multimodal dialog systems. These metrics describe system performance (e.g. in terms of error rates) and user/system interaction behavior (e.g. in terms of meta-communication acts, durations) in a quantitative way, and can thus serve as an input to the models discussed below. Input is welcome to stabilize these metrics, so that they are of more use to researchers and system developers. The proper conjunction between such metrics and standardized annotation schemes (e.g., Bunt et al., 2010) will strengthen the establishment and spreading of a specific set of metrics.

When it comes to user-perceived quality, Hone and Graham (2000) have made a first attempt to come up with a validated questionnaire (SASSI), which, however, lacks a scale to assess speech output quality. The approach has been put forward in ITU-T Rec. P.851 (2003) by including speech output and dialog managing capabilities. A framework structure was preferred over a fixed (and validated) questionnaire, in order to more flexibly address the needs of researchers and developers. This approach still needs to be extended towards multimodal systems, where modality appropriateness, preference and perceived performance have to be considered. ITU-T welcomes contributions on this topic.

For practical usage, it is desirable to have evaluation methods which provide diagnostic value to the system developer, so that the sources of misbehavior can be identified. The diagnosis can be based on perceptual dimensions (effectiveness, efficiency, mental effort, etc.) or on technical characteristics (error rates, vocabulary coverage, etc.) or both. Approaches in this direction are welcome and would significantly increase the usefulness of evaluation exercises for the system developers.

3 User-perceived Quality Prediction

The first approach to predict user judgments on the basis of interaction metrics is the well-known PARADISE model (Walker et al., 1997). The main challenge to date is the low generalizability of such models. The reason is that many of the underlying input parameters are interdependent, and that a simple linear combination does not account for more complex relationships (e.g. there might be an optimum length for a dialog, which cannot be easily described by a purely linear model).

However, other algorithms such as non-linear regression, classification trees or Markov models, have not shown a significantly improved performance (Möller et al., 2008; Engelbrecht, 2011). The latter are however adequate to describe the evolution of user opinion during the dialog, and thus might have principled advantages over models which use aggregated interaction performance metrics as an input.

4 User Behavior Simulation

During system development, it would be useful to anticipate how users would interact with a dialog system. Reflected to the system developer, such anticipations help to identify usability problems already before real users interact with the system.

Whereas user behavior simulation has frequently been used for training statistical dialog managers, only few approaches are documented which apply them to system evaluation. Early approaches mainly selected possible utterances from a set of collected data. The MeMo workbench (Engelbrecht, 2011) tried to combine statistical selection of probable interaction paths with the knowledge of usability experts about what typically influences user behavior. Such knowledge can also be generated by a conversational analysis and categorization (Schmidt et al., 2010).

A different approach has been followed in the SpeechEval project (Möller et al., 2009) where statistical dialog managers have been trained on a large diverse dataset to generate utterances on a conceptual level. The system is then amended with ASR and TTS to allow for a speech-based black-box interaction with telephone-based dialog systems. Combined with diagnostic quality prediction models, such tools can support system developers to evaluate different dialog strategies early in the design cycle and at low costs, and thus avoid dissatisfied users. The approach still has to be extended towards multimodal dialog systems.

References

Alan W Black et al, *Spoken Dialog Challenge 2010: Comparison of Live and Control Test Results*, Proc. SIGDIAL2011, Portland, OR.

H. Bunt, et al.: *Towards an ISO standard for dialogue act annotation.* Proc. LREC 2010, 19-21.

K.-P. Engelbrecht. 2011. *Estimating Spoken Dialog System Quality with User Models*, Doctoral Dissertation, TU Berlin, to appear with Springer, Berlin.

K.S. Hone, R. Graham. 2000. Towards a Tool for Subjective Assessment of Speech System Interfaces (SASSI), *Natural Language Eng.*, 6(3-4):287-303.

ITU-T Rec. P.851. 2003. *Subjective Quality Evaluation of Telephone Services Based on Spoken Dialogue Systems*, Int. Telecomm. Union, Gerneva.

ITU-T Suppl. 24 to P-Series Rec. 2005. *Parameters Describing the Interaction with Spoken Dialogue Systems*, Int. Telecomm. Union, Geneva.

ITU-T Suppl. 25 to P-Series Rec. 2011. *Parameters Describing the Interaction with Multimodal Dialogue Systems*, Int. Telecomm. Union, Geneva.

S. Möller, K.-P. Engelbrecht, R. Schleicher. 2008. Predicting the Quality and Usability of Spoken Dialogue Services, *Speech Communication* 50:730-744.

S. Möller, R. Schleicher, D. Butenkov, K.-P. Engelbrecht, F. Gödde, T. Scheffler, R. Roller, N. Reithinger. 2009. Usability Engineering for Spoken Dialogue Systems Via Statistical User Models, in: *First IWSDS 2009*, Kloster Irsee.

M.A. Walker, D.J. Litman, C.A. Kamm, A. Abella. 1997. PARADISE: A Framework for Evaluating Spoken Dialogue Agents, *Proc. ACL/EACL 35th Meeting*, Madrid, 271-280.

S. Schmidt, J. Stubbe, M. Töppel, S. Möller. 2010. Automatic Usability Evaluation for Spoken Dialog Systems Based on Rules Identified by a Sociotechnical Approach, in: *Proc. PQS 2010*, Bautzen.

Dialogue Systems Using Online Learning: Beyond Empirical Methods *

Heriberto Cuayáhuitl
German Research Center for Artificial Intelligence
Saarbrücken, Germany
hecu01@dfki.de

Nina Dethlefs
Heriot-Watt University
Edinburgh, Scotland
n.s.dethlefs@hw.ac.uk

Abstract

We discuss a change of perspective for training dialogue systems, which requires a shift from traditional empirical methods to online learning methods. We motivate the application of online learning, which provides the benefit of improving the system's behaviour continuously often after each turn or dialogue rather than after hundreds of dialogues. We describe the requirements and advances for dialogue systems with online learning, and speculate on the future of these kinds of systems.

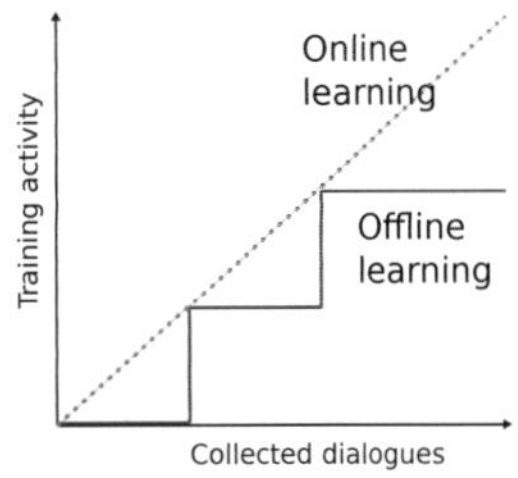

Figure 1: Learning approaches for dialogue systems. Whilst offline learning aims for discontinuous learning, online learning aims for continuous learning while interacting with users in a real environment.

1 Motivation

Important progress has been made in empirical methods for training spoken or multimodal dialogue systems over the last decade. Nevertheless, a different perspective has to be embraced if we want dialogue systems to learn on the spot while interacting with real users. Typically, empirical methods operate cyclically as follows: collect data, provide the corresponding annotations, train a statistical or other machine learning model, evaluate the performance of the learned model, and if satisfactory, deploy the trained model in a working system. The disadvantage of this approach is that while data is still being collected subsequent to deployment, the system does not optimize its behaviour anymore (cf. stepwise learning, the solid blue line in Fig. 1). In contrast, dialogue systems with online learning tackle this limitation by learning a machine learning model continuously often from unlabeled or minimally labeled data (cf. dotted red line in Fig. 1). So whilst empirical methods train models after hundreds of dialogues, online learning methods refine the system models after each user turn or each dialogue. In the rest of the paper we discuss the requirements, advances and potential future of these kind of systems.

*This research was funded by the EC's FP7 programmes under grant agreement no. ICT-248116 (ALIZ-E) and under grant agreement no. 287615 (PARLANCE).

2 Online Learning Systems: Requirements

Several requirements arise for the development of successful online learning systems. First of all, they need to employ methods that are **scalable** for real-world systems and the modelling of knowledge in sufficient detail. Second, **efficient learning** is a prerequisite for learning from an ongoing interaction without causing hesitations or pauses for the user. Third, learnt models should satisfy a **stability** criterion that guarantees that the learning agent's performance does not deteriorate over time, e.g. over the course of a number of interactions, due to the newly accumulated knowledge and behaviours. Fourth, systems should employ a **knowledge transfer** approach in which they master new tasks they are confronted with over their life span by transferring general knowledge gathered in previous tasks. Fifth, online learning sytems should adopt a **lifelong learning** approach, arguably without stopping learning. This implies making use of large data sets, which can be unlabeled or partially labeled due to the costs that they imply. Finally, in the limit of updating the learned models after every user turn, the online and offline learning methods could be the same as long as they meet the first three requirements above.

3 Online Learning Systems: Advances

Several authors have recognised the potential benefits of online learning methods in previous work.

Thrun (1994) presents a robot for lifelong learning that learns to navigate in an unknown office environment by suggesting to transfer general purpose knowledge across tasks. Bohus et al. (2006) describe a spoken dialogue system that learns to optimise its non-understanding recovery strategies online through interactions with human users based on pre-trained logistic regression models. Cuayáhuitl and Dethlefs (2011) present a dialogue system in the navigation domain that is based on hierarchical reinforcement learning and Bayesian Networks and relearns its behaviour after each user turn, using indirect feedback from the user's performance. Gašić et al. (2011) present a spoken dialogue system based on Gaussian Process-based Reinforcement Learning. It learns directly from binary feedback that users assign explicitly as rewards at the end of each dialogue and that indicate whether users were happy or unhappy with the system's performance. From these previous investigations, we can observe that online learning systems can take both explicit and/or implicit feedback to refine their trained models.

4 Online Learning Systems: Future

While previous work has made important steps, the problem of lifelong learning for spoken dialogue systems is far from solved. Especially the following challenges will need to receive attention: (a) fast learning algorithms that can retrain behaviours after each user turn with stable performance; and (b) scalable methods for optimizing multitasked behaviours at different levels and modalities of communication.

In addition, we envision online learning systems with the capability of transfering knowledge across systems and domains. For example: a dialogue act classifier, an interaction strategy, or a generation strategy can be made transferable to similar tasks. This could involve reasoning mechanisms to infer what is known/unknown based on past experiences. The idea of learning from scratch every time a new system is constructed will thus be avoided. In this regard, the role of the system developer in these kinds of systems is not only to specify the system's tasks and learning environment, but to constrain and bootstrap the system behaviour for faster learning. All of these capabilities will be possible using online learning with a lifelong learning perspective.

5 Tools and Data

Currently there are software tools for training models but they are more suitable for offline learning.[1] Software tools for online learning remain to be developed and shared with the community. In addition, since building a dialogue system typically requires a tremendous amount of effort, researchers working on learning approaches should agree on standards to facilitate system development. Finally, since dialogue data is an often lacking resource in the community, the online learning perspective may contribute towards reducing the typical chicken and egg problem, due to dialogue knowledge being more readily transferable across domains, subject to online adaption towards particular domains.

References

Dan Bohus, Brian Langner, Antoine Raux, Alan Black, Maxine Eskenazi, and Alexander Rudnicky. 2006. Online Supervised Learning of Non-Understanding Recovery Policies. In *Proc. IEEE SLT*.

Heriberto Cuayáhuitl and Nina Dethlefs. 2011. Optimizing Situated Dialogue Management in Unknown Environments. In *Proc. INTERSPEECH*.

Milica Gašić, Filip Jurčíček, Blaise Thomson, Kai Yu, and Steve Young. 2011. On-line policy optimisation of spoken dialogue systems via interaction with human subjects. In *Proc. IEEE ASRU*.

Sebastian Thrun. 1994. A Lifelong Learning Perspective for Mobile Robot Control. In *Proc. IEEE/RSJ/GI*.

[1] www.cs.waikato.ac.nz/ml/weka/

Statistical User Simulation for Spoken Dialogue Systems: What for, Which Data, Which Future? *

Olivier Pietquin
SUPELEC - UMI 2958 (GeorgiaTech - CNRS)
2 rue Edouard Belin
57070 Metz - France
olivier.pietquin@supelec.fr

Abstract

There has been a lot of interest for user simulation in the field of spoken dialogue systems during the last decades. User simulation was first proposed to assess the performance of SDS before a public release. Since the late 90's, user simulation is also used for dialogue management optimisation. In this position paper, we focus on statistical methods for user simulation, their main advantages and drawbacks. We initiate a reflection about the utility of such methods and give some insights of what their future should be.

1 Introduction

User simulation for Spoken Dialogue Systems (SDS) aims at generating artificial interactions supposed to be representative of what would be an actual dialogue between a human user and a given dialogue system. User simulation is thus different from user modeling which is often included into the systems to infer user goals from observable clues (user's utterances, intonations etc.) (Zukerman and Albrecht, 2001). In this paper we focus on statistical methods for user simulation, that is methods purely based on data and statistical models and not cognitive models. Also, we only address user simulations working at the intention level, that is generating dialog acts and not speech or natural language (Schatzmann et al., 2006). User modeling, used to infer user intentions in dialogue systems is not addressed.

*This work as been partially funded by the INTERREG IVa project ALLEGRO and the Région Lorraine

The aim of user simulation was initially to assess the performance of a SDS before a public release (Eckert et al., 1997). Given a performance metric and a simulation method, the natural idea of automatically optimizing SDS (using reinforcement learning RL) appeared in the literature in the late 90's (Levin et al., 2000).

2 Is user simulation useful?

Initially, SDS optimisation required a lot of data because of inefficiency of RL algorithms, justifying the use of simulation. In recent years, sample efficient RL methods were applied to SDS optimization. This allows learning optimal dialogue strategies directly from batches of data collected between suboptimal systems and actual users (Li et al., 2009; Pietquin et al., 2011b) but also from online interactions (Pietquin et al., 2011a; Gasic et al., 2011). Do we have to conclude that user simulation is useless?

3 Do we need to train models?

It is commonly admitted that learning parameters of user simulation models is hard because most of variables are hidden (user goal, mental states etc.) and tricky to annotate. This is why current user simulators are trainable but rarely trained (Pietquin, 2006; Schatzmann et al., 2007). Do we really need to train user simulation models? If so, which data and annotation schemes do we need?

4 Does simulation reach the target?

User simulation aims at reproducing plausible interactions but in contexts that were not seen in the data collected to train the model. It is generally hard to assess the quality of such models. Especially, it is hard to find a single metric to assess user simulation performances (Pietquin and Hastie, 2011). Also, it has been shown that user simulation affects a lot the result of SDS strategy optimisation (Schatzmann et al., 2005). What should be assessed? Statistical consistency, ability to generalize, ability to generate sequences of interactions similar to real dialogues, ability to produce optimal strategies by RL? If one wants to learn an optimal simulation model, there is a need for a single optimality criterion.

5 What's the future of user simulation for SDS?

Whatever the use one wants to make of user simulation (learning or assessment for SDS), the future of this research field relies probably on a redefinition of the role of user simulation. So far, user simulation is seen as a generative systems, generating dialog acts according to the context. Current user simulation models are therefore based on a large amount of conditional probabilities which are hard to learn, and the training (if there is one) requires a lot of prior knowledge, the introduction of smoothing parameters etc.

We believe that user simulation should be redefined as a sequential decision making problem in which a user tries to reach a goal in a natural and efficient way, helped by an artificial agent (the SDS). One major difference between this vision and the common probabilistic one is that it takes into account the fact that human users adapt their behavior to the performances and the strategy of the SDS. This can be called "co-adaptation" between human users and artificial systems and justifies that user simulation should still be studied.

Recently, user simulation models based on inverse reinforcement learning have been proposed (Chandramohan et al., 2011). In this framework, a user is modeled as optimizing it's behavior according to some unknown reward which is inferred from recorded data. This might be an answer to the co-adaptation problem. Yet, is user simulation still useful in this framework? Knowing the reward of the user, do we still need simulation or is it possible to compute directly an optimal dialogue strategy?

References

S. Chandramohan, M. Geist, F. Lefèvre, and O. Pietquin. 2011. User Simulation in Dialogue Systems using Inverse Reinforcement Learning. In *Proc. of Interspeech 2011*, Florence (Italy).

W. Eckert, E. Levin, and R. Pieraccini. 1997. User Modeling for Spoken Dialogue System Evaluation. In *Proc. of ASRU'97*, Santa Barbara (USA).

M. Gasic, F. Jurcicek, B. Thomson, K. Yu, and S. Young. 2011. On-line policy optimisation of spoken dialogue systems via live interaction with human subjects". In *Proc. of ASRU 2011*, Hawaii (USA).

E. Levin, R. Pieraccini, and W. Eckert. 2000. A Stochastic Model of Human-Machine Interaction for learning dialog Strategies. *IEEE Transactions on Speech and Audio Processing*, 8:11–23.

L. Li, S. Balakrishnan, and J. Williams. 2009. Reinforcement Learning for Dialog Management using Least-Squares Policy Iteration and Fast Feature Selection. In *Proc. of InterSpeech'09*, Brighton (UK).

O. Pietquin and H. Hastie. 2011. A survey on metrics for the evaluation of user simulations. *Knowledge Engineering Review*.

O. Pietquin, M. Geist, and S. Chandramohan. 2011a. Sample Efficient On-line Learning of Optimal Dialogue Policies with Kalman Temporal Differences. In *Proc. of IJCAI 2011*, Barcelona, Spain.

O. Pietquin, M. Geist, S. Chandramohan, and H. Frezza-Buet. 2011b. Sample-Efficient Batch Reinforcement Learning for Dialogue Management Optimization. *ACM Transactions on Speech and Language Processing*, 7(3):7:1–7:21, May.

O. Pietquin. 2006. Consistent goal-directed user model for realistic man-machine task-oriented spoken dialogue simulation. In *ICME'06*, Toronto (Canada).

J. Schatzmann, M.Stuttle, K. Weilhammer, and S. Young. 2005. Effects of the user model on simulation-based learning of dialogue strategies. In *Proc. of ASRU'05.*

J. Schatzmann, K. Weilhammer, M. Stuttle, and S. Young. 2006. A survey of statistical user simulation techniques for reinforcement-learning of dialogue management strategies. *Knowledge Engineering Review, vol. 21(2), pp. 97–126.*

J. Schatzmann, B. Thomson, K. Weilhammer, H. Ye, and S. Young. 2007. Agenda-based User Simulation for Bootstrapping a POMDP Dialogue System. In *Proc. of HLT NAACL.*

I. Zukerman and D. Albrecht. 2001. Predictive statistical models for user modeling. *User Modeling and User-Adapted Interaction*, 11(1-2):5–18. invited paper.

The Future of Spoken Dialogue Systems is in their Past: Long-Term Adaptive, Conversational Assistants

David Schlangen
Faculty of Linguistics and Literary Studies
Bielefeld University, Germany
david.schlangen@uni-bielefeld.de

Abstract

A sketch of dialogue systems as long-term adaptive, conversational agents.

1 Introduction

"*Show me the lecture notes from last year*", you say to your bow-tied virtual assistant. It does, but unfortunately, "*this will not do. Pull up all the new articles I haven't read yet*". Your assistant obliges, pointing your attention to a "*new article from your friend, Jill Gilbert*". A video call later, your lecture preparation is done—Jill will actually give it, via video link—and you go on with your day.

This of course describes the first scene from Apple's "Knowledge Navigator" concept video (Apple Computer Inc., 1987; Colligan, 2011). Not much of what that video showed was actually technically possible at the time, but it captured the promise of personalized natural language interfaces that many people saw and hoped would be realised soon. Having to deal with the constraints of reality, however, research and development of spoken dialogue interfaces had to set itself the more modest aim of replacing, in certain settings, mouse and keyboard, rather than personal assistants.

Recent years have seen two developments that bring that more ambitious goal back into focus. First, the required basic technologies such as speech recognition and speech synthesis have matured to a state where they begin to allow the necessary flexibility of spoken in- and output. Second, it has become not only possible but completely unremarkable for large portion of the population to carry with them sensor-rich, networked computing devices—their smartphones—during large parts of their day.

In this position paper, I'd like to sketch what the opportunities are that this situation offers, for the creation of dialogue systems that are *long-term adaptive* and *conversational*, and act as *assistants*, not interfaces.

2 Long-Term Adaptive ...

The fact that users carry with them the same device (or class of devices; it only matters that access is constant), provides the chance of repeated interactions with what is understood to be the same system. To make use of this, the system must

- learn from errors / miscommunications, by improving internal models (acoustic model, language model, semantic models: how are tasks structured for particular user); and it must
- build up personal common ground:

– What has been refered to previously, and how? Which tasks have been done together, and how?
– Which situations have been shared? (Where a multi-sensor device can have detailed situational information.)

While the first point mostly describes current practice (user adaptation of speech resources), there is much to be explored in the building up of common ground with a technical device.

3 ... Conversational ...

Interaction with these systems must be less driven by fixed system-intiative, and be more conversational:

- User and system must be able to mean more than they say, by making use of context, both from the ongoing conversation as well as from the common ground that was built up over previous interaction.

• Systems should be responsive, incremental, providing feedback where required; realising a tight interaction loop, not strict turn-based exchanges.

• Things will go wrong, so error handling needs to be graceful and natural, using the full range of conversational repair devices (Schlangen, 2004; Purver, 2004); including handing off tasks to other modalities if expected success rate is low.

• Conversations express and project personality, emotionality, sociality; systems need to model the dynamics of this as part of their modelling of the conversation.

Again, these are active areas of research (for responsive systems, see e.g. (Skantze and Schlangen, 2009; Buß et al., 2010; Schlangen et al., 2010); for error handling / acting under uncertainty, see e.g. (Williams and Young, 2007); for social aspects of dialogue, see e.g. (Kopp, 2010)); pulling them together in this kind of application will likely provide new challenges and insights for all of them.

4 ... Assistants

Of course, the systems will need to provide actual services, for it at all to come to repeated conversations. While providing the services lies outside the domain of speech research, there are some unique requirements that conversational access poses:

• To be usefully embeddable into conversational systems, back-end applications are needed that are interaction-ready; e.g., by providing confindence information about their results, and, building on this, by suggesting ways to improve quality through additional information.

• Not all back-end services are under the control of the application developer or provide APIs, and the semantic web is not going to happen. The reach of a virtual assistant can be increased if it can be *taught* to do tasks like use a website to book a train. Some promising first work in this direction exists (Allen et al., 2007).

5 Resources

Building dialogue systems is always hard, as many different components need to be integrated. Systems as sketched above bring the additional challenge of requiring work on mobile platforms; a framework that provides the required interfaces and infrastructure would be very helpful.

References

James F. Allen, Nathanael Chambers, George Ferguson, Lucian Galescu, Hyuckchul Jung, Mary Swift, and William Taysom. 2007. PLOW: A collaborative task learning agent. In *Proceedings of the National Conference on Artificial Intelligens (AAAI)*, Vancouver, BC, Canada.

Apple Computer Inc. 1987. The knowledge navigator concept video. http://youtu.be/HGYFEI6uLy0.

Okko Buß, Timo Baumann, and David Schlangen. 2010. Collaborating on utterances with a spoken dialogue system using an isu-based approach to incremental dialogue management. In *Proceedings of the SIGdial 2010 Conference*, pages 233–236, Tokyo, Japan, September.

Bud Colligan. 2011. How the knowledge navigator video came about, Nov. http://www.dubberly.com/articles/how-the-knowledge-navigator-video-came-about.html.

Stefan Kopp. 2010. Social resonance and embodied coordination in face-to-face conversation with artificial interlocutors. *Speech Communication*, 52(6):587–597.

Matthew Purver. 2004. *The Theory and Use of Clarification Requests in Dialogue*. Ph.D. thesis, King's College, Unversity of London, London, UK, August.

David Schlangen, Timo Baumann, Hendrik Buschmeier, Okko Buß, Stefan Kopp, Gabriel Skantze, and Ramin Yaghoubzadeh. 2010. Middleware for incremental processing in conversational agents. In *Proceedings of the SIGdial 2010 Conference*, pages 51–54, Tokyo, Japan, September.

David Schlangen. 2004. Causes and strategies for requesting clarification in dialogue. In *Proceedings of the 5th Workshop of the ACL SIG on Discourse and Dialogue*, Boston, USA, April.

Gabriel Skantze and David Schlangen. 2009. Incremental dialogue processing in a micro-domain. In *Proceedings of the 12th Conference of the European Chapter of the Association for Computational Linguistics (EACL 2009)*, pages 745–753, Athens, Greece, March.

Jason Williams and Steve Young. 2007. Partially observable Markov decision processes for spoken dialog systems. *Computer Speech and Language*, 21(2):231–422.

Towards Situated Collaboration

Dan Bohus, Ece Kamar, Eric Horvitz
Microsoft Research
One Microsoft Way
Redmond, WA, 98052, USA
{dbohus,eckamar,horvitz@microsoft.com}

Abstract

We outline a set of key challenges for dialog management in physically situated interactive systems, and propose a core shift in perspective that places spoken dialog in the context of the larger collaborative challenge of managing parallel, coordinated actions in the open world.

Multiple models for dialog management have been proposed, studied, and evaluated in the research community (*i.a.* Allen et al, 2001; Bohus and Rudnicky, 2009; Rich and Sidner, 1998; Traum and Larsson, 2003; Williams and Young, 2007). In the process, a diverse set of problems have come to light and have been pursued. These include the challenges of modeling initiative in interaction, contextual interpretation and processing, the management of uncertainty, grounding, error handling and recovery, turn-taking and, more recently, incremental processing in dialog systems. Analyses of existing approaches (Allen et. al, 2001; Churcher et. al, 1997; McTear 2002; Paek and Pieraccini, 2008) reveal a constellation of benefits but also shortcomings along multiple dimensions, where no single technique provides the benefits of all.

While taking incremental, focused steps is important for making progress within a mature discipline, we believe that the current scope and conceptual borders of work in spoken dialog constrains thinking about possibilities and gets in the way of achieving breakthrough advances. Research to date on dialog management has focused almost exclusively on dyadic settings, where *a single user* interacts with a system over a relatively narrow, *speech-only* channel. Characteristics of this dominant and shared worldview on dialog research have driven modeling and architectural choices, and often done so in an implicit, hidden manner. For instance, dialog is often viewed as a collection of dialog moves that are timed in a relatively well-structured, sequential fashion. As a consequence, dialog management models typically operate on a "per-turn" basis: inputs are assumed to arrive sequentially and are processed one at a time; for each received input, discourse understanding is performed, and a corresponding response is generated.

In reality, interactions among actors situated in the open, physical world depart deeply from common assumptions made in spoken dialog research and bring into focus an array of important, new challenges (Horvitz, 2007; Bohus and Horvitz, 2010; Bohus, Horvitz, Kanda et al., eds., 2010). We describe some of the challenges with respect to dialog management, and re-frame this problem as an instance of the larger collaborative challenge of managing parallel, coordinated actions amidst a dynamically changing physical world.

As an example, consider a robot that has been given the responsibility of greeting, interacting, and escorting visitors in a building. In this setting, reasoning about the actors, objects and events and relationships in the scene can play a critical role in understanding and organizing the interactions. The surrounding environment provides *rich, continuously streaming situational context* that is relevant for determining the best way an agent might contribute to interactions. Because the situational context can evolve asynchronously with respect to turns in the conversation, systems that operate in the open world must be able to *plan continuously, in stream*, rather than on a "per-turn" basis. Interaction and collaboration in these settings is best viewed as a flow of *coordinated, parallel actions*. The sequential structure of turns in dyadic interactions is but one example of such coordination, focused solely on linguistic actions. However, to successfully interact and collaborate with multiple participants in physically situated settings, an agent must be able to recognize, plan, and produce both linguistic and non-linguistic actions, and reason about potentially complex patterns of coordination between actions, *in-stream*—as they are being produced by the participants in the collaboration.

We argue that attaining the dream of fluid, seamless spoken language interaction with machines requires a fundamental shift in how we view dialog management. First, we need to move from *per-turn* to continual *in-stream* planning. Second, we need to move from reasoning about *sequential* actions to reasoning about *parallel and coordinated* actions and their influence on states in the world. And third, we need models that can *track and leverage the streaming situational context*, from noisy observations, to make decisions about how to best contribute to collaborations.

Spoken dialog is an important channel for expressing coordinative information. However, we need to recognize and begin to tackle head on the larger challenge of *situated collaborative activity management*. We understand that taking this perspective introduces new complexities—and that some of our colleagues will view diving into the larger problems in advance of solving simpler ones as being unwise. However, we believe that we must embrace the larger goals to make significant progress on the struggles with the simpler ones, and that the investment in solving challenges with physically situated collaboration will have eventual payoffs in enabling progress in spoken dialog.

Making progress on the broader challenge requires technical innovations, tools, and data. Consider for instance one sub-problem of belief tracking in these systems: continuously updating beliefs over the state of the collaborative activity and the situational context requires the development of new types of models that can combine streaming evidence about context collected through sensors, with discrete evidence about the actions performed or the turns spoken collected through speech, gesture or other action-recognition components. In addition, progress hinges on identifying a set of relevant problem domains, and coordinating efforts in the community to collect data, and comparatively evaluate proposed approaches. New tools geared towards analysis, visualization and debugging with streaming multimodal data are also required.

We propose a core shift of perspective and associated research agenda for moving from *dialog management* to *situated collaborative activity management*. We invite discussion on these ideas.

References

Allen, J.F., Byron, D.K., Dzikovska, M., Ferguson, G., Galescu, L., and Stent, A. 2001. Towards Conversational Human-Computer Interaction, *AI Magazine*, **22**(3)

Bohus, D., and Rudnicky, A. 2009. The Ravenclaw dialog management framework: Architecture and systems, in *Computer, Speech and Language*, **23**(3).

Bohus, D., and Horvitz, E. 2010. On the Challenges and Opportunities of Physically Situated Dialog, *AAAI Symposium on Dialog with Robots*, Arlington, VA.

Bohus, D., Horvitz, E., Kanda, T., Mutlu, B., Raux, A., editors, 2010. Special Issue on "Dialog with Robots", *AI Magazine* **32**(4).

Churcher, G. E., Atwell, E.S, and Souter, C. 1997 Dialogue Management Systems: a Survey and Overview, *Technical Report*, University of Leeds, Leeds, UK.

Horvitz, E., 2007. Reflections on Challenges and Promises of Mixed-Initiative Interaction, *AI Magazine* 28, pp. 19-22.

McTear, M.F. 2002. Spoken dialogue technology: enabling the conversational user interface, *ACM Computing Surveys,* **34**(1):90-169.

Paek, T., and Pierracini, R. 2008. Automating Spoken Dialogue Management design using machine learning: An industry perspective, *Speech Communication*, **50**(8-9):716-729.

Rich, C., and Sidner, C.L. 1998. Collagen: A Collaboration Manager for a Collaborative Interface Agent, *User Modelling and User Assisted Interaction,* **7**(3-4):315-350, Kluwer Academic Publishers.

Traum, D., and Larsson, S. 2003. The Information State Approach to Dialogue Management. *Current and New Directions in Discourse and Dialogue*, Text Speech and Language Technology, **22:**325-353.

Williams, J., and Young, S., 2007. Partially Observable Markov Decisions Processes for Spoken Dialog Systems, *Computer, Speech and Language*, **21**(2).

Young, S. 2006. Using POMDPs for Dialog Management, in *Proc. of SLT-2006*, Palm Beach, Aruba.

Incremental Spoken Dialogue Systems: Tools and Data

Helen Hastie, Oliver Lemon, Nina Dethlefs
The Interaction Lab, School of Mathematics and Computer Science
Heriot-Watt University, Edinburgh, UK EH14 4AS
h.hastie, o.lemon, n.s.dethlefs@hw.ac.uk

Abstract

Strict-turn taking models of dialogue do not accurately model human incremental processing, where users can process partial input and plan partial utterances in parallel. We discuss the current state of the art in incremental systems and propose tools and data required for further advances in the field of Incremental Spoken Dialogue Systems.

1 Incremental Spoken Dialogue Systems

For Spoken Dialogue Systems (SDS) to be more frequently adopted, advances in the state-of-the-art are necessary to enable highly responsive and conversational systems. Traditionally, the unit of speech has been a whole utterance with strict, rigid turn-taking determined by a voice-activity detector. However, a large body of psycholinguistic literature indicates that human-human interaction is in fact incremental (Tanenhaus and Brown-Schmidt, 2008; Levelt, 1989). Using a whole utterance as the unit of choice makes dialogues longer, unnatural and stilted and ultimately interferes with a user's ability to focus on their goal (Allen et al., 2001).

A new generation of Incremental SDS (ISDS) are being developed that deal with 'micro-turns' (sub-utterance processing units) resulting in dialogues that are more fluid and responsive. Recent work has shown that processing smaller 'chunks' of input and output can improve the user experience (Aist et al., 2007; Skantze and Schlangen, 2009; Buss et al., 2010; Baumann et al., 2011; Selfridge et al., 2011). Incrementality enables the system designer to model several dialogue phenomena that play a vital role in human discourse (Levelt, 1989) but have so far been absent from systems. These include more natural turn-taking through rapid system responses, grounding through the generation of backchannels and feedback, and barge-ins (from both user and system). In addition, corrections and self-corrections through constant monitoring of user and system utterances play an important role, enabling the system to recover smoothly from a recognition error or a change in user's preferences. Some examples of the phenomena we are targeting are given in Figure 1.

Parlance, a FP7 EC project[1], is currently developing incremental systems for English and Mandarin. The goal of Parlance is to develop mobile, interactive, 'hyper-local' search through speech. Recent trends in Information Retrieval are towards incremental, interactive search. Spoken dialogue systems can provide a truly natural medium for this type of search, in particular for people on the move.

2 Tools and Data

The emphasis of the Parlance project is on data-driven techniques for ISDS, thereby addressing the problem of a lack of data for system development. Although incremental dialogue phenomena described in Figure 1 have been observed in human-human dialogue, more task-based data is needed. It is challenging to fabricate a situation where users produce incremental discourse phenomena as in Figure 1 frequently and in a natural manner. Wizard-

[1] http://www.parlance-project.eu

Backchannels (when the user pauses)

USR I want Italian food [500 ms] in the centre of town ...
SYS uh-huh
SYS OK. I found 24 Italian restaurants in the city centre. The restaurant *Roma* is in the medium price range,...

Self-correction (the system made a mistake)

USR I want Italian food in the centre of town ...
SYS OK. I found 35 Indian restaurants ...
USR No, I want Italian.
SYS oh sorry ...
SYS I have 24 Italian restaurants in the city centre ...

Holding the floor

USR I want cheap Italian food ...
SYS ok let me see
SYS I have 3 cheap Italian places ...

Figure 1: Incremental phenomena observed in human-human dialogue that systems should be able to model.

of-Oz experiments can be used to collect data from the system side, but user-initiated phenomena, such as the user changing his/her mind are more difficult to instigate. Therefore, data collections of naturally occurring incremental phenomena in human-human settings will be essential for further development of incremental systems. Such data can inform user simulations which provide means of training stochastic SDS with less initial data and can compensate for data sparsity. For example, in Dethlefs et al. (2012) the user simulation can change its mind and react to different NLG strategies such as giving information with partial input or waiting for complete input from the user. Both the academic community and industry would benefit from open access data, such as will be collected in the Parlance project and made available to the dialogue community[2]. There would also need to be a clear path from academic research on ISDS to industry standards such as VoiceXML to facilitate adoption.

Various components and techniques of ISDS are needed to handle 'micro-turns'. Challenges here include recognizing and understanding partial user input and back-channels; micro-turn dialogue management that can decide when to back-channel, self-correct and hold-the-floor; incremental NLG that can generate output while the user is still talking; and finally more flexible TTS that can handle barge-in and understand when it has been interrupted.

In summary, in order to achieve highly natural, responsive incremental systems, we propose using data-driven techniques, for which the main issue is lack of data. Carefully crafted task-based human-human data collection and WoZ studies, user simulations, shared data archives, and upgraded industry standards are required for future work in this field.

Acknowledgments

The research leading to this work has received funding from the EC's FP7 programme: (FP7/2011-14) under grant agreement no. 287615 (PARLANCE).

References

Gregory Aist, James Allen, Ellen Campana, Lucian Galescu, Carlos Gomez Gallo, Scott Stoness, Mary Swift, and Michael Tanenhaus. 2007. Software architectures for incremental understanding of human speech. In *Proceedings of SemDial / DECALOG*.

James Allen, George Ferguson, and Amanda Stent. 2001. An Architecture For More Realistic Conversational Systems. In *Proc. of Intelligent User Interfaces*.

Timo Baumann, Okko Buss, and David Schlangen. 2011. Evaluation and Optimisation of Incremental Processors. *Dialogue and Discourse*, 2(1).

Okko Buss, Timo Baumann, and David Schlangen. 2010. Collaborating on Utterances with a Spoken Dialogue Systen Using an ISU-based Approach to Incremental Dialogue Management. In *Proc. of SIGDIAL*.

Nina Dethlefs, Helen Hastie, Verena Rieser, and Oliver Lemon. 2012. Optimising Incremental Generation for Spoken Dialogue Systems: Reducing the Need for Fillers. In *Proc of INLG*, Chicago, Illinois, USA.

Willem Levelt. 1989. *Speaking: From Intenion to Articulation*. MIT Press.

Ethan Selfridge, Iker Arizmendi, Peter Heeman, and Jason Williams. 2011. Stability and Accuracy in Incremental Speech Recognition. In *Proc. of SigDial*.

Gabriel Skantze and David Schlangen. 2009. Incremental Dialogue Processing in a Micro-Domain. In *Proc. of EACL*, Athens, Greece.

M.K. Tanenhaus and S. Brown-Schmidt. 2008. Language processing in the natural world. In B.C.M Moore, L.K. Tyler, and W.D. Marslen-Wilson, editors, *The perception of speech: from sound to meaning*, pages 1105–1122.

[2]As was done for CLASSiC project data at: http://www.macs.hw.ac.uk/iLabArchive/CLASSiCProject/Data/login.php

After Dialog Went Pervasive: Separating Dialog Behavior Modeling and Task Modeling

Amanda J. Stent
AT&T Labs - Research
Florham Park, NJ 07932, USA
stent@research.att.com

Dialog Goes Pervasive Until recently, many dialog systems were *information retrieval* systems. For example, using a telephone-based interactive response system a US-based user can find flights from United (1-800-UNITED-1), get movie schedules (1-800-777-FILM), or get bus information (Black et al., 2011). These systems save companies money and help users access information 24/7. However, the interaction between user and system is tightly constrained. For the most part, each system only deals with one domain, so the task models are typically flat slot-filling models (Allen et al., 2001b). Also, the dialogs are very structured, with system initiative and short user responses, giving limited scope to study important phenomena such as coreference.

Smart phones and other mobile devices make possible *pervasive* human-computer spoken dialog. For example, the Vlingo system lets users do web searches (information retrieval), but also connects calls, opens other apps, and permits voice dictation of emails or social media updates[1]. Siri can also help users make reservations and schedule meetings[2].

These new dialog systems are different from traditional ones in several ways; they are *multi-task, asynchronous, can involve rich context modeling*, and have *side effects in the "real world"*:
Multi-task – The system interacts with the user to accomplish a series of (possibly related) tasks. For example, a user might use the system to order a book and then say *schedule it for book club* - a different task (e.g. requiring different backend DB lookups) but related to the previous one by the book information. Multi-task interaction increases the difficulty of interpretation and task inference, and so requires new kinds of dialog model (e.g. (Lison, 2011)).
Asynchronous – the user may give the system a command (e.g. *Add Hunger Games with Mary for 3 pm*), and the system may follow up on that command an hour later, after considerable intervening dialog (e.g. *Mary texted you about the Hunger Games*). Because the dialog is multi-task, it is more free-flowing, with less clear start and end points but more opportunities for adaptation and personalization.
Rich context modeling – Mobile devices come with numerous sensors useful for collecting non-linguistic context (e.g. GPS, camera, web browser actions), while the semi-continuous nature of the interaction permits collection of rich linguistic context. So far, dialog systems have used this context only in limited ways (e.g. speech recognizer personalization). However, the opportunities for modeling human interaction behavior, including multimodal interaction, are tremendous.
Side effects "in the real world" – the system (with input from the user) can cause changes in the state of the world (e.g. emails get sent, hotel rooms get booked). This increases the importance of grounding and agreement in the interaction. But it enables new kinds of evaluation, for example based on the number of successfully completed subtasks over time, or on comparing the efficacy of alternative system behaviors with the same user.

Dialog Challenges and Task Challenges The implications for research on dialog systems are clear. It is unsustainable to reimplement dialog behaviors for each new task, or limit the use of context to the

[1] www.vlingo.com
[2] http://www.apple.com/iphone/features/siri.html

most basic semantic representations. As the field moves forward, *dialog behavior modeling will be increasingly separated from task modeling* (Allen et al., 2001a; Allen et al., 2001b). Research on dialog modeling will focus on dialog *layers*, task-independent dialog behaviors such as (incremental) turn-taking, grounding, and coreference that involve both participants. Research on task modeling can focus on the design of task models that are agnostic to the types or forms of interaction that will use them, on general models for interactive problem-solving (Blaylock and Allen, 2005), and on rapid acquisition and adaptation of task models (Jung et al., 2009).

Within this space, there can be two types of (collaborative or competitive) "dialog challenge":
Dialog layer-focused – Participants focus on models for a particular dialog behavior, such as turn-taking, grounding, alignment, or coreference. Implementations cover both the interpretation and the generation aspects of the behavior. Evaluation may be based on a comparison of the implemented behaviors to human language behaviors (e.g. for turn-taking, inter-turn silence, turn-final and turn-initial prosodic cues), and/or on user error rates and satisfaction scores. An initial dialog layer-focused challenge could be on turn-taking (Baumann and Schlangen, 2011; Selfridge and Heeman, 2010).
Task modeling focused – This type of challenge will move from modeling individual tasks, to automatic acquisition and use of task models for interactive tasks in dialog systems. Future challenges of this type would build on this by incorporating (in order): (a) tasks other than information retrieval (e.g. survey tasks (Stent et al., 2008)); (b) task completion (tasks with subtasks that have side effects, e.g. purchasing a ticket after looking up a route); (c) task adaptation (during development, participants work with one task, and during evaluation, participants work with a different but related task); and (d) multi-task modeling. Participating systems could learn by doing (Jung et al., 2009), via user simulation (Rieser and Lemon, 2011), from corpora (Bangalore and Stent, 2009), or from scripts or other abstract task representations (Barbosa et al., 2011).

Tools for the Community It has never been easier (with a little Web programming) to rapidly prototype dialog systems as mobile apps, or to use them to collect data. To enable researchers to focus on dialog- and task-modeling rather than component development, AT&T is happy to offer its AT&T WATSON^{SM} speech recognizer and Natural Voices^{TM} text-to-speech synthesis engine in the cloud, through its Speech Mashup platform (Di Fabbrizio et al., 2009), to participants in dialog challenges. The Speech Mashup supports rich logging of both linguistic and non-linguistic context, and is freely available at *http://service.research.att.com/smm*.

References

J. F. Allen, G. Ferguson, and A. Stent. 2001a. An architecture for more realistic conversational systems. In *Proceedings of IUI.*

J. F. Allen et al. 2001b. Towards conversational human-computer interaction. *AI Magazine*, 22(4):27–37.

S. Bangalore and A. Stent. 2009. Incremental parsing models for dialog task structure. In *Proceedings of EACL.*

L. Barbosa et al. 2011. SpeechForms - from web to speech and back. In *Proceedings of Interspeech.*

T. Baumann and D. Schlangen. 2011. Predicting the micro-timing of user input for an incremental spoken dialogue system that completes a user's ongoing turn. In *Proceedings of SIGDIAL.*

A. W. Black et al. 2011. Spoken dialog challenge 2010: comparison of live and control test results. In *Proceedings of SIGDIAL.*

N. Blaylock and J. F. Allen. 2005. A collaborative problem-solving model of dialogue. In *Proceedings of SIGDIAL.*

G. Di Fabbrizio, T. Okken, and J. Wilpon. 2009. A speech mashup framework for multimodal mobile services. In *Proceedings of ICMI-MLMI.*

H. Jung et al. 2009. Going beyond PBD: A play-by-play and mixed-initiative approach. In *Proceedings of the CHI Workshop on End User Programming for the Web.*

P. Lison. 2011. Multi-policy dialogue management. In *Proceedings of SIGDIAL.*

V. Rieser and O. Lemon. 2011. Learning and evaluation of dialogue strategies for new applications: Empirical methods for optimization from small data sets. *Computational Linguistics*, 37(1):153–196.

E. Selfridge and P. Heeman. 2010. Importance-driven turn-bidding for spoken dialogue systems. In *Proceedings of ACL.*

A. Stent, S. Stenchikova, and M. Marge. 2006. Dialog systems for surveys: The Rate-A-Course system. In *Proceedings of SLT.*

Future Directions in Spoken Dialog Systems: A Community of Possibilities

Alan W Black and Maxine Eskenazi
Language Technologies Institute,
Carnegie Mellon University, Pittsburgh, PA, USA
{awb,max}@cs.cmu.edu

Abstract

A spoken dialog system consists of a number of non-trivially interacting components. In order to allow new students, researchers and developers to meaningfully and relatively rapidly enter the field it is critical that, despite their complexity, the resources be accessible and easy to use. Everyone should be able to start building new technologies without spending a significant amount of time re-inventing the wheel. There are four levels of support that we believe new entrants should have. 1) A flexible open source system that runs on many different operating systems, is well documented and supports both simple and complex dialog systems. 2) Logs and speech files from a large number of dialogs that enable analysis and training of new systems and techniques. 3) An actual set of real users that speak to the system on a regular basis. 4) The ability to run studies on complete real user platforms.

1 Background

The goal of the Dialog Research Center (DialRC) has been to provide the spoken dialog community with three levels of support in the form of tools and data for spoken dialog systems: open source software; logs and speech data from real dialogs, a community of real users that use a system regularly on real, useful platforms on which researchers can run studies. In this short paper we describe these four elements that our Center has endeavored to provide. Looking to the future we look to the spoken dialog community to contribute other platforms to ours to give newcomers to the field a rich set of experimental platforms on which to learn the ropes.

Open source spoken dialog software: We already provide, as Open Source software, the CMU Olympus Spoken Dialog System that offers ASR, TTS, a Dialog Manager and other components that allow developers to build both simple and complex dialog systems. While this architecture has been used in many systems (some of them are: TeamTalk [Harris et al 2004], RavenCalendar [Stenchikova et al. 2007], ConQuest [Bohus et al. 2007] and Let's Go [Raux et al. 2006]), it needs to be accompanied by more support in the form of both documentation and flexibility. It should also not be the only platform that is available to the community to run studies. There are new students, researchers and developers who want to hone their skills by adapting a dialog architecture and running it on a real user platform. In order to make it easier for these newcomers to build dialog systems in the form of short homework assignments (perhaps in 1-2 weeks), for a regular class, Olympus must be more flexible, and easier to understand and master.

With the open source core system that has already been released, we plan to add virtual machines that have all of the components preinstalled, as done in another area by [Tokuda et al 2012]. This will make it easier for newcomers to start writing and modifying dialog systems immediately rather than spending time installing black box software. This implies that our existing Windows support must be extended to also cover Linux and Mac OSX.

Log data from dialogs: Some of the significant, exciting advances that have recently been seen in the realm of spoken dialog systems use statistical modeling. This implies the acute need for data, above all *real data*, to train the models. The platforms that provide that data to a community should follow a standardized format in the same way that speech files have become standardized. Log Data can be used for offline analysis that, in turn, can afford deeper first hand insight into how spoken dialog systems.

A community of real users and real platforms to run studies: we have seen [Young, 2010] that it is no longer reasonable to test a hypothesis about spoken dialog with a small number of paid participants. End users must be real: they have some interest in the outcome of the task at hand and they are not using the system just because they're paid and/or collecting evaluation data. This goal is difficult. However, we at DialRC want to provide a centralized mechanism to give the newcomers (and already established researchers as well) access to a group of platforms with real users. There must be the possibility of obtaining a tangible benefit from these real platforms and the research community should be willing to open their systems to others so that they can test their ideas in a realistic context, with a significant number of real callers.

Our current efforts have often centered on classic telephone-based information giving systems. Going forward it is important to take a wider view of the types of spoken dialog research we can address. Thus we are also interested in supporting: multimodal interaction, human-robot interaction, multi-party communication and even tasks with no clear definition of task completion (e.g. conversational banter). What is important is not promoting one type of research more than another. It is making many different real-user platforms available to the community at large.

CMU's DialRC proposes to act as a clearing house for software (our own and that of any others), data (both speech and logfiles), and runtime real application/real user platforms that gives the community a central place to find a platform that corresponds to their needs, to connect them to the developers of that platform, and to help distribute the data (speech and logfiles) coming from their use of it.

These three actions will build communities of new researchers and developers who, from their use of this plethora of platforms will enrich the latter with what they have learned and will enrich our community with their presence.

We envisage the following scenario. A student has a short assignment to make some change to one of the basic architectures that has been made available by DialRC. When the assignment is finished, they link their system to a platform that they found through our central listing. Real users call that platform (here, our student's system) when they need what is being offered (information on a good vegetarian restaurant in Cambridge, when the next bus to the airport is coming in Pittsburgh, a discussion of new things to see in a museum, etc). The student can then access the real user data that has been collected while their version of the system was running. Perhaps in a following assignment, if they provided two versions of the system, they can find out, from analyzing the data, which condition worked best. If they provided one condition, and other students provided other ones, then they can compare their results to those of the other students.

A constantly available resource, the competition between versions of a system does not have to be held at a time that may be inconvenient for some. It can be an ongoing event that researchers can participate in when it is convenient for them to do so.

References

Harris, T., Banerjee, S., Rudnicky, A., Sison, J., Bodine, K., and Black, A. (2004) "A Research Platform for Multi-Agent Dialogue Dynamics", IEEE Workshop on Robotics and Human Interactive Communication.

Stenchikova, S., Mucha, B., Hoffman, S., Stent, A. (2007), "RavenCalendar: A Multimodal Dialog System for Managing a Personal Calendar". HLT-NAACL 2007.

Bohus, B., Grau, S, Huggins-Danes, D., Keri, V., Anumachipalli, G., Kumar, R., Raux, A. & Tomko, S. (2007) "ConQuest: an Open-Source Dialog System for Conferences", HLT-NAACL 2007.

Raux, A., Langner, B., Bohus, D., Black, A., and Exkenazi, M. (2005) "Let's Go Public! Taking a Spoken Dialog System to the Real World." Interspeech 2005.

Tokuda, K, Lee, A, Yamagishi, J. et al. (2012) "Spoken Dialog system Framework based on User Generated Content", Nagoya Institute of Technology, and University of Edinburgh, funded under JST CREST Program.

Young, S. "Still Talking to Machines (Cognitively Speaking), Keynote Interspeech 2010, Makuhari Japan.

Bridging Gaps for Spoken Dialog System Frameworks in Instructional Settings

Gina-Anne Levow
Department of Linguistics
University of Washington
Seattle, WA 98195 USA
levow@u.washington.edu

Abstract

Spoken dialog systems frameworks fill a crucial role in the spoken dialog systems community by providing resources to lower barriers to entry. However, different user groups have different requirements and expectations for such systems. Here, we consider the particular needs for spoken dialog systems toolkits within an instructional setting. We discuss the challenges for existing systems in meeting these needs and propose strategies to overcome them.

1 Introduction

A key need in the spoken dialog systems community is a spoken dialog system development framework. Such systems fulfill fundamental roles in lowering barriers to entry for development of spoken dialog systems, providing baseline systems for comparability, and supporting novel experimental extensions. There are many characteristics that are desirable for a shared spoken dialog system resource, including:

- Availability: Systems should be provided on an on-going basis, with continuing support, updates, and maintenance.
- Ease-of-use: Systems should be easy to use and provide an environment in which systems are easy to develop.
- Platform-independence: Systems be usable on a wide variety of architectures, if installed, or provided on an accessible platform, such as a website.
- Application access: Systems should provide a range of exemplar applications within the framework.
- Flexibility and extensibility: Systems should enable integration of diverse technology components and facilitate a wide range of experimental configurations.
- Robustness: Systems should enable state-of-the-art performance for diverse applications.
- Affordability: Systems should be free if possible, or provided at pricing that is not prohibitive for different user groups.

However, these systems also serve diverse groups of users, from senior research developers to students building their first spoken dialog systems. While these users share many requirements, their relative importance naturally varies. Research developers will likely place greater emphasis on system robustness, extensibility, and flexibility, for example to incorporate alternative speech recognizers, speech synthesizers, or dialog managers. Those using such systems in an instructional setting will place greater importance on ease-of-use, platform portability or independence, availability, affordability, and access to reference applications. Below, we will discuss some of the challenges for systems trying to meet these needs. Then we will describe two popular current solutions and how they satisfy the needs of these different groups. Lastly we will present some additional needs for spoken dialog systems frameworks to bridge gaps in dialog systems for instructional use.

A variety of systems have been developed that address many of these needs, but all suffer from significant limitations. Availability and affordability have posed some of the knottiest problems. For example, many of the Galaxy Communicator research systems, such as those by University of Colorado (Pellom et al., 2001), MIT, and CMU, were made available to the research community. However, many of the systems are no longer available, usable, or supported, as research groups have disbanded and systems architectures have changed. Maintaining systems over time requires group and community commitment, facilitated by an open-source framework. Other toolkits and frameworks have become problematic due to conflicts between availability and affordability. The long-popular CSLU toolkit (Sutton and Cole, 1997) has recently shifted to a commercial footing. Similarly, several industry platforms have provided free non-commercial VoiceXML hosting, as a simple spoken dialog development environment. However, at least one of these systems has recently shifted to a paid-only status. The environment changes rapidly. Of three freely available academic systems and five VoiceXML platforms listed in a 2009 survey (Jokinen and McTear, 2009), two have already gone to paid status as of late 2011.

Two frameworks have emerged in recent years as popular SDS frameworks: the Ravenclaw/Olympus framework (Bohus et al., 2007) and VoiceXML, hosted on one of the industrial platforms, such as Nuance's Cafe or Voxeo[1]. However, they do seem to address the needs of different user groups. Ravenclaw/Olympus has been more widely adopted in the research community: it is robust, flexible, extensible, open-source, provides diverse use cases, and has an active support and development community. In contrast, the VoiceXML platforms have proven popular in an instructional setting, as attested by the large number of online homework assignments employing VoiceXML. These VoiceXML frameworks offer very simple, easy-to-use environments that are largely platform-independent, include basic support and tutorials, and provide simple baseline applications. Given VoiceXML's extensive role in industry settings, they also provide an advantage in terms of direct practical experience for students and in terms of broad resources and support. In an instructional setting, Ravenclaw/Olympus' relative complexity, Windows platform and software dependence in instructional environments where linux has become predominant, and smaller resource base represent hurdles. While the VoiceXML platforms excel in these dimensions, their very simplicity and ease-of-use are limiting. Students are often looking for existing applications of moderate interesting complexity as a basis for extension and experimentation. Most typical example applications are simpler than those given for Olympus, and the platform is severely limiting for more advanced users and tasks. For example, many VoiceXML frameworks do not even support user-defined pronunciations. Lastly, these VoiceXML platforms rely on the generosity of the industrial teams, which can readily evaporate as has already happened with Tellme Studio.

Ideally, for instructional use, we would like to bridge the gap between the too-simple, restrictive VoiceXML frameworks and the more challenging but more flexible and powerful Ravenclaw/Olympus framework, to allow students and instructors to transition more smoothly from one to the other. On the VoiceXML side, a community-supported VoiceXML platform would reduce dependence on industry platforms. Access to VoiceXML applications of greater complexity, comparable to Let's Go! or Communicator tasks, would allow more interesting experiments within a course's limited span. Lastly, porting Ravenclaw/Olympus to linux would allow easier adoption in a wider range of academic programs.

[1] http://cafe.bevocal.com; http://www.voxeo.com

References

D. Bohus, Antoine Raux, Thomas K. Harris, Maxine Eskenazi, and Alexander I. Rudnicky. 2007. Olympus: an open-source framework for conversational spoken language interface research. In *Bridging the Gap: Academic and Industrial Research in Dialog Technology workshop at HLT/NAACL 2007.*

Kristiina Jokinen and Michael F. McTear. 2009. *Spoken Dialogue Systems.* Morgan & Claypool Publishers.

B. Pellom, W. Ward, J. Hansen, K. Hacioglu, J. Zhang, X. Yu, and S. Pradhan. 2001. University of Colorado dialog systems for travel and navigation.

Stephen Sutton and Ronald Cole. 1997. The cslu toolkit: rapid prototyping of spoken language systems. In *Proceedings of the 10th annual ACM symposium on User interface software and technology*, UIST '97, pages 85–86, New York, NY, USA. ACM.

A belief tracking challenge task for spoken dialog systems

Jason D. Williams
Microsoft Research, Redmond, WA 98052 USA
jason.williams@microsoft.com

Abstract

Belief tracking is a promising technique for adding robustness to spoken dialog systems, but current research is fractured across different teams, techniques, and domains. This paper amplifies past informal discussions (Raux, 2011) to call for a *belief tracking challenge* task, based on the *Spoken dialog challenge* corpus (Black et al., 2011). Benefits, limitations, evaluation design issues, and next steps are presented.

1 Introduction and background

In dialog systems, *belief tracking* refers to maintaining a distribution over multiple dialog states as a dialog progresses. Belief tracking is desirable because it provides robustness to errors in speech recognition, which can be quite common.

This distribution can be modeled in a variety of ways, including heuristic scores (Higashinaka et al., 2003), Bayesian networks (Paek and Horvitz, 2000; Williams and Young, 2007), and discriminative models (Bohus and Rudnicky, 2006). Techniques have been fielded which scale to realistically sized dialog problems and operate in real time (Young et al., 2009; Thomson and Young, 2010; Williams, 2010; Mehta et al., 2010). In lab settings, belief tracking has been shown to improve overall system performance (Young et al., 2009; Thomson and Young, 2010).

Despite this progress, there are still important unresolved issues. For example, a deployment with real callers (Williams, 2011) found that belief tracking sometimes degraded performance due to model mis-matches that are difficult to anticipate at training time. What is lacking is a careful comparison of methods to determine their relative strengths, in terms of generalization, sample efficiency, speed, etc.

This position paper argues for a belief tracking challenge task. A corpus of labeled dialogs and scoring code would be released. Research teams would enter one or more belief tracking algorithms, which would be evaluated on a held-out test set.

2 Corpus

The *Spoken dialog challenge* corpus is an attractive corpus for this challenge. It consists of phone calls from real (not simulated) bus riders with real (not imagined) information needs. There have been 2 rounds of the challenge (2010, and 2011-2012), with 3 systems in each round. The rounds differed in scope and (probably) user population. A total of 3 different teams entered systems, using different dialog designs, speech recognizers, and audio output. For each system in each round, 500-1500 dialogs were logged. While it would be ideal if the corpus included more complex interactions such as negotiations, as a publicly available corpus it is unparalleled in terms of size, realism, and system diversity.

There are limitations to a challenge based on this corpus: it would not allow comparisons across domains, nor for multi-modal or situated dialog. These aspects could be left for a future challenge. Another possible objection is that off-line experiments would not measure end-to-end impact on a real dialog system; however, we do know that good belief tracking improves dialog performance (Young et al., 2009; Thomson and Young, 2010; Williams, 2011), so characterizing and improving belief tracking seems a logical next step. Moreover, building an end-to-end dialog system is a daunting task, out of reach of many research teams without specific funding. A corpus-based challenge has a much lower barrier to entry.

3 Evaluation issues

There are many (not one!) metrics to evaluate. It is crucial to design these in advance and implement them as computer programs for use during development. Specific metrics could draw on the following core concepts. **Baseline accuracy** measures the speech recognition 1-best – i.e., accuracy without belief tracking. **1-best accuracy** measures how often the belief tracker's 1-best hypothesis is correct. **Mean reciprocal rank** measures the quality of the ordering of the belief state, ignoring the probabilities used to order; **log-likelihood** measures the quality of the probabilities. **ROC curves** measure the 1-best discrimination of the belief tracker at different false-accept rates, or at the **equal error rate**.

An important question is *at which turns* to assess the accuracy of the belief in a slot. For example, accuracy could be measured at every turn; every turn after a slot is first mentioned; only turns where a slot is mentioned; only turns where a slot appears in the speech recognition result; and so on. Depending on the evaluation metric, it may be necessary to annotate dialogs for the user's goal, which could be done automatically or manually. Another issue is how to automatically determine whether a belief state value is correct at the semantic level.

A final question is how to divide the corpus into a training and test set in a way that measures robustness to the different conditions. Perhaps some of the data from the second round (which has not yet been released) could be held back for evaluation.

4 Next steps

The next step is to form a group of interested researchers to work through the issues above, particularly for the preparation of the corpus and evaluation methodology. Once this is documented and agreed, code to perform the evaluation can be developed, and additional labelling (if needed) can be started.

Acknowledgments

Thanks to Antoine Raux for advocating for this challenge task, and for helpful discussions. Thanks also to Spoken Dialog Challenge organizers Alan Black and Maxine Eskenazi.

References

AW W Black, S Burger, A Conkie, H Hastie, S Keizer, O Lemon, N Merigaud, G Parent, G Schubiner, B Thomson, JD Williams, K Yu, SJ Young, and M Eskenazi. 2011. Spoken dialog challenge 2010: Comparison of live and control test results. In *Proc SIGdial Workshop on Discourse and Dialogue, Portland, Oregon.*

D Bohus and AI Rudnicky. 2006. A 'K hypotheses + other' belief updating model. In *Proc AAAI Workshop on Statistical and Empirical Approaches for Spoken Dialogue Systems, Boston.*

H Higashinaka, M Nakano, and K Aikawa. 2003. Corpus-based discourse understanding in spoken dialogue systems. In *Proc ACL, Sapporo.*

N Mehta, R Gupta, A Raux, D Ramachandran, and S Krawczyk. 2010. Probabilistic ontology trees for belief tracking in dialog systems. In *Proc SIGdial Workshop on Discourse and Dialogue, Tokyo, Japan.*

T Paek and E Horvitz. 2000. Conversation as action under uncertainty. In *Proc Conf on Uncertainty in Artificial Intelligence (UAI), Stanford, California*, pages 455–464.

A Raux. 2011. Informal meeting on a belief tracking challenge at interspeech.

B Thomson and SJ Young. 2010. Bayesian update of dialogue state: A POMDP framework for spoken dialogue systems. *Computer Speech and Language*, 24(4):562–588.

JD Williams and SJ Young. 2007. Partially observable Markov decision processes for spoken dialog systems. *Computer Speech and Language*, 21(2):393–422.

JD Williams. 2010. Incremental Partition Recombiantion for Efficient Tracking of Multiple Dialogue States. In *ICASSP*, Dallas, TX.

JD Williams. 2011. An empirical evaluation of a statistical dialog system in public use. In *Proc SIGDIAL, Portland, Oregon, USA.*

SJ Young, M Gašić, S Keizer, F Mairesse, J Schatzmann, B Thomson, and K Yu. 2009. The hidden information state model: a practical framework for POMDP-based spoken dialogue management. *Computer Speech and Language.*

Framework for the Development of Spoken Dialogue System based on Collaboratively Constructed Semantic Resources

Masahiro Araki **Daisuke Takegoshi**
Department of Information Science
Kyoto Institute of Technology
Matsugasaki Sakyo-ku Kyoto 6068585 Japan
araki@kit.ac.jp

Abstract

We herein introduce our project of realizing a framework for the development of a spoken dialogue system based on collaboratively constructed semantic resources. We demonstrate that a semantic Web-oriented approach based on collaboratively constructed semantic resources significantly reduces troublesome rule descriptions and complex configurations, which are caused by the previous relational database-based approach, in the development process of spoken dialogue systems. In addition, we show that the proposed framework enables multilingual spoken dialogue system development due to clear separation of model, view and controller components.

1 Introduction

In recent years, some large scale repositories of collaboratively constructed semantic resources (CSRs), such as Freebase[1], are available online. Those semantically structured data enable more precise search than simple text matching (e.g. "Find a dental clinic near Kyoto station opens at Saturday night.") and more complex search than simple query to relational database (RDB) (e.g. a query "Find machine learning books written by a researcher of NLP." needs cross search on a book DB and a researcher DB). Since search conditions of such queries to the structured data become complex, natural language, especially speech, for smart phone and tablet PC, is a promising method of query input.

There are some previous researches on converting natural language input to the query of structured data (Lopez et al., 2006) (Tablan et al., 2008). These researches basically concentrated on the input sentence analysis and the query construction. If the developer want to apply existing natural language understanding methods to spoken dialogue system (SDS) for structured data search, there remains fair amount of components that need to be implemented, such as speech input component, dialogue flow management, backend interface, etc.

In order to realize a development environment of SDS for structured data search, we designed a data model driven framework for rapid prototyping of SDS based on CSRs. The proposed framework can be regarded as an extension of existing Rails framework of Web application to (1) enabling speech interaction and (2) utilizing a benefit of CSRs. By using CSRs and the extended Rails framework, the troublesome definitions of rules and templates for SDS prototyping can be reduced significantly compared with the ordinary RDB-based approach.

As this data model driven approach is independent of language for interaction, the proposed framework has a capability of easily implementing multilingual SDS.

[1] http://www.freebase.com/

The remainder of the present paper is organized as follows. Section 2 describes the proposed approach to a data modeling driven development process for SDS based on CSRs and explains the automatic construction of the spoken query understanding component. Section 3 demonstrates the multilingual capability of the proposed framework. In Section 4, the present paper is concluded, and a discussion of future research is presented.

2 Data modeling driven approach based on CSRs

2.1 Object-oriented SDS development framework

We previously proposed a data modeling driven framework for rapid prototyping of SDS (Araki 2011). We designed a class library that is based on class hierarchy and attribute definitions of an existing semantic Web ontology, i.e., Schema.org[2]. This class library is used as a base class of an application-specific class definition. An example of class definition is shown in Figure 1.

```
@DBSearch
@SystemInitiative
class MyBook extends Book {
  Integer ranking
  static constraints = {
    name(onsearch:"like")
    author(onsearch:"like")
    publisher()
    ranking(number:true)
  }
}
```

Figure 1: Example of class definition.

In this example, the "MyBook" class inherits all of the attributes of the "Book" class of Schema.org in the same manner as object-oriented programming languages. The developer can limit the attributes that are used in the target application by listing them in the constraints section of the class definition. On the other hand, the developer can add additional attributes (*ranking* attributes as the type of *Integer*, which is not defined in original "Book" class) in the definition of the class.

The task type and dialogue initiative type are indicated as annotations at the beginning of the class definition. In this example, the task type is *DB search* and the initiative type is *user initiative*. This information is used in generating the controller code (state transition code, which is equivalent to Figure 2) and view codes of the target SDS.

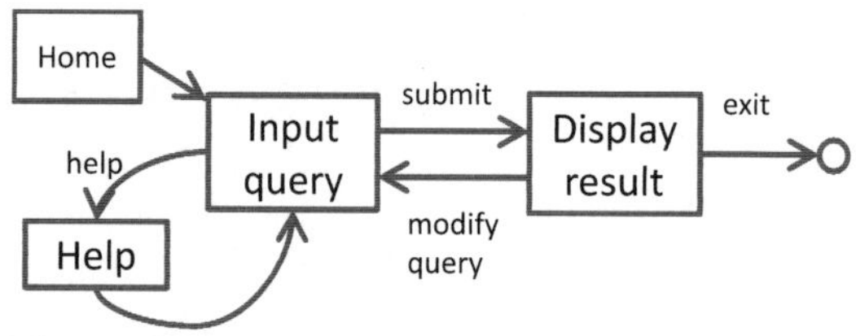

Figure 2: Control flow of the DB search task.

Using Grails[3], which is a Rails Web application framework, the proposed framework generates the dialogue controller code of the indicated task type and the view codes, which have speech interaction capability on the HTML5 code from this class definition. The overall concept of the data modeling driven framework is shown in Figure 3.

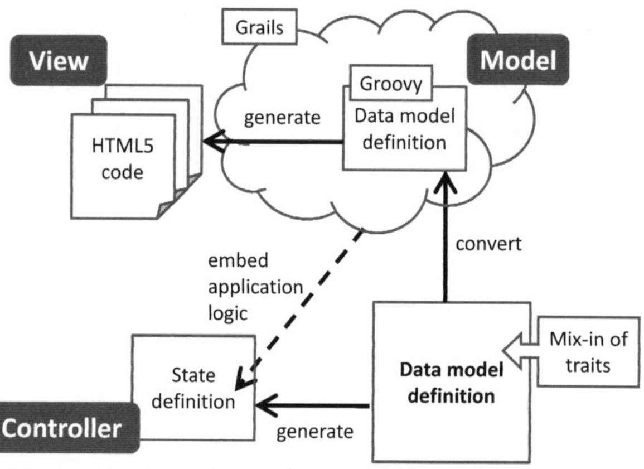

Figure 3: Overview of the data modeling driven SDS development framework.

2.2 Using CSRs

The disadvantage of our previous framework, described in the previous subsection, is the high dependence on the dictation performance of the speech recognition component. The automatically generated HTML5 code invokes dictation API, irrespective of the state of the dialogue and initiative type. In order to improve speech recognition accuracy, grammar rules (in system initiative dialogue) and/or the use of a task/domain-dependent language model (in mixed/user initiative dialogue)

[2] http://schama.org/

[3] http://grails.org/

are key factors. In our previous framework, the developer had to prepare these ASR-related components using language resources, which are beyond the proposed data-driven framework.

In order to overcome this defect, we add the Freebase class library, which is based on large-scale CSRs, because Freebase already includes the contents of the data. These contents and a large-scale Web corpus facilitate the construction of grammar rules and a language model that is specific to the target task/domain.

For example, the Film class of Freebase has more than 191 thousand entries (as of May 2012), most of which have information about directors, cast members, genres, etc. These real data can be used as resources to improve ASR accuracy.

In system initiative type dialogue, the contents of each attribute of the target class can construct word entries of the grammar rule for each attribute slot. For example, the grammar rule for the user's response to "Which genre of movie are you searching for?" can be constructed from the contents of the genres attribute of the Film class. We implemented a generator of the set of content words specified in the data model definition from the data of Freebase. The generator is embedded as one component of the proposed framework.

In the mixed/user initiative type tasks, since content words and functional words make up the user's utterance, we need a language model for speech recognition and a semantic frame extractor for the construction of query to semantic data. We designed and implemented a language model generator and a semantic frame extractor using a functional expression dictionary that corresponds to the attributes of Freebase (Araki submitted). The flow of the language model generation is shown in Figure 4.

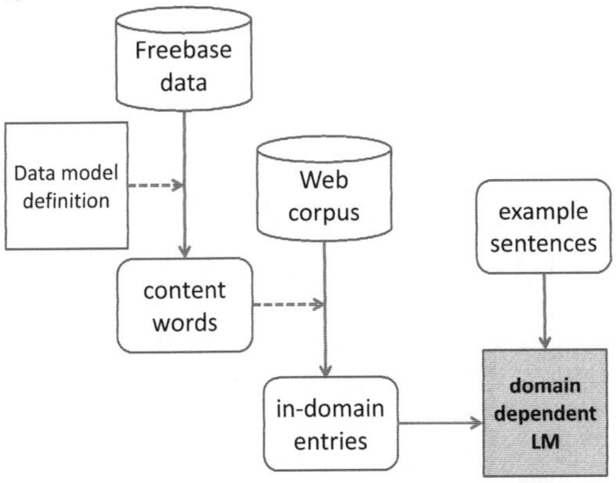

Figure 4: Construction process of LM.

2.3 Helper application for data definition

In order to facilitate the data-model definition process, we implemented a helper application called MrailsBuilder. A screenshot of one phase of the definition process is shown in Figure 5, which shows the necessary slots for data definition in the GUI and a list of properties once the developer selects the parent class of the target class.

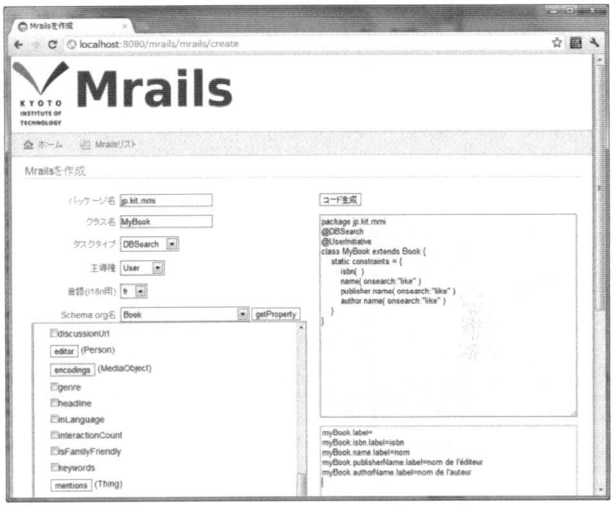

Figure 5: Screenshot of MrailsBuilder.

3 Multilingual extension of the framework

With the internationalization capability of the Grails base framework and multilingual data resources provided as CSRs, we can generate a multilingual SDS from the data model definition. All of the language-dependent information is stored in separated property files and is called at the time of the dynamic view code generation process in the interaction, as shown in Figure 6.

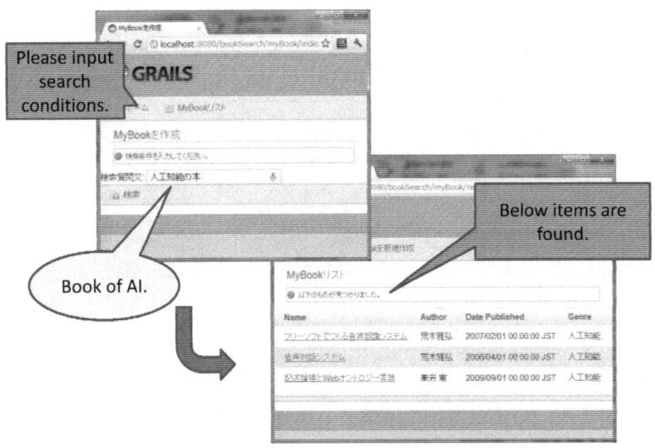

Figure 6: Example of realized interaction.

We also implemented a *contents extractor* from Freebase data. In Freebase, each class (called "type") belongs to one domain. For example, the "Dish" type belongs to the "Food & Drink" domain (see Figure 7). Although it assigned to a two-level hierarchy, each type has no inherited properties. Therefore, it is easy for Freebase data to represent a set of property values as a string instead of a uniform resource identifier (URI). Each instance has the name property and its value is written in English. For some instances, it also has the name description in another language with the language code. Therefore, we can extract the name of the instance in various languages.

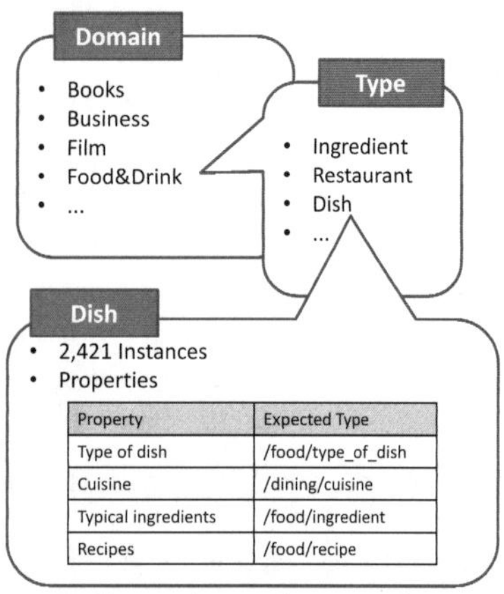

Figure 7: Domain and type of Freebase.

The input of the *contents extractor* is the model definition code as in Figure 1 and the language code (e.g., "ja" for Japanese). As an example, the "MyDish" class is defined as shown in Figure 8.

```
@DBSearch
@UserInitiative
class MyDish extends Dish {
  static constraints = {
    name()
    type_of_dish1(nullable:true)
    cuisine(nullable:true)
    ingredients(nullable:true)
    recipes(nullable:true)
  }
}
```

Figure 8: Model definition of the "MyDish" class.

The *contents extractor* outputs the instance records of the given language code and this instance can be used for LM generator explained in section 2.2. For example, the extracted words in the case of "de" (German) is shown in Figures 9.

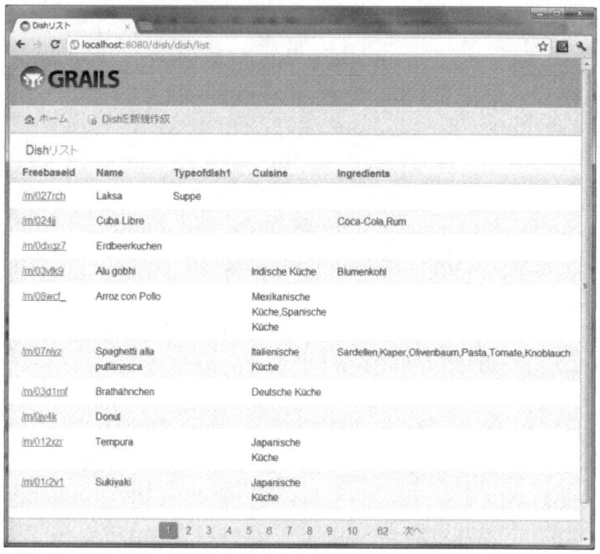

Figure 9: German contents of the "MyDish" class.

4 Conclusions and future research

We have proposed a framework for development of a SDS on CSRs and have explained rapid construction method of spoken query understanding component and showed its multilingual capability.

In future research, we plan to evaluate the quantitative productivity of the proposed framework.

Acknowledgments

The present research was supported in part by the Ministry of Education, Science, Sports, and Culture through a Grant-in-Aid for Scientific Research (C), 22500153, 2010.

References

Masahiro Araki and Yuko Mizukami. 2011. Development of a Data-driven Framework for Multimodal Interactive Systems. In Proc. of IWSDS 2011, 91-101.

Masahiro Araki and Daisuke Takegoshi. accepted. A Rapid Development Framework for Multilingual Spoken Dialogue Systems. In Proc. of IEEE COMPSAC 2012.

Masahiro Araki. submitted. An Automatic Construction Method of Spoken Query Understanding Component from Data Model Definition.

Vanessa Lopez, Enrico Motta, and Victoria S. Uren. 2006, AquaLog: An ontology-driven Question Answering System to interface the Semantic Web. In Proc. of HLT-NAACL 2006, 269-272.

Valentin Tablan, Danica Damljanovic, and Kalina Bontcheva. 2008, A natural language query interface to structured information. In Proc. of the 5h European Semantic Web Conference (ESWC 2008).

The INPROTK 2012 Release

Timo Baumann
Department for Informatics
University of Hamburg, Germany
baumann@informatik.uni-hamburg.de

David Schlangen
Faculty of Linguistics and Literary Studies
Bielefeld University, Germany
david.schlangen@uni-bielefeld.de

Abstract

We describe the 2012 release of our "Incremental Processing Toolkit" (INPROTK)[1], which combines a powerful and extensible architecture for incremental processing with components for incremental speech recognition and, new to this release, incremental speech synthesis. These components work fairly domain-independently; we also provide example implementations of higher-level components such as natural language understanding and dialogue management that are somewhat more tied to a particular domain. We offer this release of the toolkit to foster research in this new and exciting area, which promises to help increase the naturalness of behaviours that can be modelled in such systems.

1 Introduction

As recent work has shown, incremental (or *online*) processing of user input or generation of system output enables spoken dialogue systems to produce behaviour that is perceived as more natural than and preferable to that produced by systems that are bound by a turn-based processing mode (Aist et al., 2006; Skantze and Schlangen, 2009; Buß et al., 2010; Skantze and Hjalmarsson, 2010). There is still much left to find out about the best ways of modelling these behaviours in such systems, however. To foster research in this area, we are releasing a new version of our "Incremental Processing Toolkit" (INPROTK), which provides lower-level components (such as speech recognition and speech synthesis, but also a general modular processing architecture) and allows researchers to concentrate on higher-level modules (such as natural language understanding and dialogue modelling; for which we provide example implementations).[2] We describe these components in the following, pointing out the differences and extensions to earlier releases (Baumann et al., 2010).

2 An Incremental Processing Architecture

INPROTK realises the *IU*-model of incremental processing (Schlangen and Skantze, 2009; Schlangen and Skantze, 2011), where incremental systems are conceptualised as consisting of a network of processing *modules*. Each module has a *left buffer*, a *processor*, and a *right buffer*, where the normal mode of processing is to take input from the left buffer, process it, and provide output in the right buffer, from where it goes to the next module's left buffer. (Top-down, expectation-based processing would work in the opposite direction.) Modules exchange *incremental units* (IUs), which are the smallest 'chunks' of information that can trigger connected modules into action. IUs typically are part of larger units; e.g., individual words as parts of an utterance, or frame elements as part of the representation of an utterance meaning. This relation of being part of the same larger unit is recorded through *same level links*; the units that were used in creating a given IU are linked to it via *grounded in* links. Modules have to be able to react to three basic situations: that IUs are *added* to a buffer, which triggers processing; that IUs that were erroneously hypothesised by an earlier module

[1]The code of the toolkit and some example applications have been released as open-source at http://inprotk.sourceforge.net.

[2]An alternative to the toolkit described here is *jindigo* (Skantze and Hjalmarsson, 2010), http://www.jindigo.net.

are *revoked*, which may trigger a revision of a module's own output; and that modules signal that they *commit* to an IU, that is, won't revoke it anymore (or, respectively, expect it to not be revoked anymore).

INPROTK offers flexibility on how tightly or loosely modules are coupled in a system. It provides mechanisms for sending IU updates between processes via a light-weight remote procedure call protocol,[3] as well as for using shared memory within one (Java) process. INPROTK follows an event-based model, where modules create events, for which other modules can register as listeners. Module networks are configured via a system configuration file which specifies which modules *listen* to which.

As opposed to our previous release (Baumann et al., 2010), INPROTK module communication is now completely encapsulated in the `IUModule` class. An implementing processor is called into action by a method which gives access both to the edits to IUs in the left buffer since the last call, and to the list of IUs directly. The implementing processor must then notify its right buffer, either about the edits to the right buffer, or giving the content directly. Modules can be fully event-driven, only triggered into action by being notified of a hypothesis change, or they can run persistently, in order to create endogenous events like time-outs. Event-driven modules can run concurrently in separate threads or can be called sequentially by another module (which may seem to run counter the spirit of incremental processing, but can be advantageous for very quick computations for which the overhead of creating threads should be avoided). In the case of separate threads, which run at different update intervals, the left-buffer view will automatically be updated to its most recent state.

INPROTK also comes with an extensive set of monitoring and profiling modules which can be linked into the module network at any point and allow to stream data to disk or to visualise it online through a viewing tool (von der Malsburg et al., 2009), as well as different ways to simulate input (e.g., typed or read from a file) for debugging. All IUmodules can also output loggging messages to the viewing tool directly (to ease graphic debugging of error cases in multi-threaded applications).

[3]In an earlier release, we used OAA (Cheyer and Martin, 2001), which however turned out to be too slow.

3 Incremental Speech Recognition

Our speech recognition module is based on the Sphinx-4 (Walker et al., 2004) toolkit and comes with acoustic models for German.[4] The module queries the ASR's current best hypothesis after each frame of audio and changes its output accordingly, adding or revoking `WordIUs` and notifying its listeners. Additionally, for each of the WordIUs, `SyllableIUs` and `SegmentIUs` are created and bound to the word (and to the syllable respectively) via the grounded-in hierarchy. Later modules in the pipeline are thus able to use this lower-level information (e.g. to disambiguate meaning based on prosodic aspects of words). For *prosodic processing*, we inject additional processors into Sphinx' acoustic frontend which provide features for further prosodic processing (pitch, loudness, and spectral tilt). In this way, IUs are able to access the precise acoustic data (in raw and processed forms).

An ASR's current best hypothesis frequently changes during the recognition process with the majority of the changes not improving the result. Every such change triggers all listening modules (and possibly their listeners), resulting in a lot of unnecessary processing. Furthermore, changes may actually deteriorate results, if a 'good' hypothesis is intermittently changed for worse. Therefore, we developed *hypothesis smoothing* approaches (Baumann et al., 2009) which greatly reduce spurious edits in the output at the cost of some timeliness: With a lag of 320 ms we reduced the amount of spurious edits to 10 % from an initial 90 %. The current implementation of hypothesis smoothing is taylored specifically towards ASR output, but other input modules (like gesture or facial expression recognition) could easily be smoothed with similar methods.

4 Incremental NLU and DM

As mentioned above, the more "higher-level" components in our toolkit are more domain-specific than the other components, and in any case are probably exactly those modules which users of the toolkit may want to substitute with their own. Nevertheless, we provide example implementations of a simple keyword-spotting 'NLU', as well as statistically

[4]Models for English, French and other languages are available from the Sphinx' distribution and from `http://www.voxforge.org`.

trained ones (Schlangen et al., 2009; Heintze et al., 2010).

We have recently built a somewhat more traditional NLU component which could be more easily ported to other domains (by adapting lexicon and grammar). It consists of a probabilistic, beam-search top-down parser (following (Roark, 2001)), which produces a principled semantic representation in the formalism *robust minimal recursion semantics* (Copestake, 2006). This component is described in more detail in (Peldszus et al., 2012).

5 Incremental Speech Synthesis

Rounding out the toolkit is our new component for incremental speech synthesis, which has the following properties:

(a) It makes possible changes to the as-yet unspoken part of the ongoing utterance,

(b) allows adaptations of delivery parameters such as speaking rate or pitch with very low latency.

(c) It autonomously makes delivery-related decisions (such as producing hesitations), and

(d) it provides information about delivery status (e. g. useful in case of barge-ins).

(e) And, last but not least, it runs in real time.

Figure 1 provides a look into the internal data structures of the component, showing a triangular structure where on successive levels structure is built *just-in-time* (e.g., turning target phoneme sequences into vocoding parameters) and hence can be changed with low cost, if necessary. We have evaluated the component in an application scenario where it proved to increase perceived naturalness, and have also studied the tradeoff between look-ahead and prosodic quality. To this end, Figure 2 plots the deviation of the prosodic parameters *pitch* and *timing* from that of a non-incremental synthesis of the same utterance versus the amount of *look-ahead*, that is, how far into the current phrase the next phrase becomes known. It shows that best results are achieved if the next phrase that is to be synthesized becomes known no later than one or two words into the current phrase (w_0 or w_1).

6 Evaluation of Incremental Processors

While not part of the toolkit proper, we think that it can only be useful for the field to agree on common evaluation metrics. Incremental processing brings new considerations of dynamics into the assessment of processing quality, and hence requires additional metrics compared to non-incremental processing. In (Baumann et al., 2011) we have proposed a family of such metrics, and we provide an evaluation framework for analysing incremental ASR performance as part of our distribution.

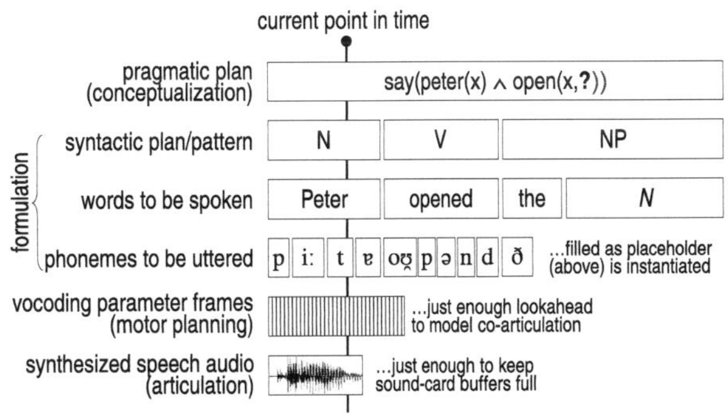

Figure 1: Hierarchic structure of incremental units describing an example utterance as it is being produced during delivery, showing the event-based just-in-time processing strategy.

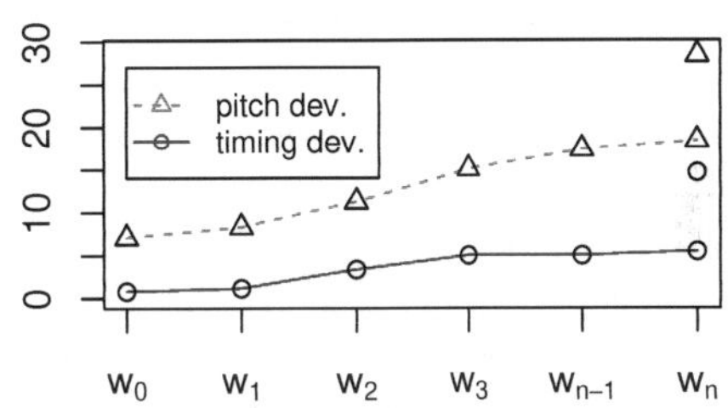

Figure 2: Deviation of pitch and timing plotted against lookahead (right context available for incremental synthesis). The more lookahead available, the better the results.

7 Conclusions

We have sketched the major features of our "Incremental Processing Toolkit" INPROTK. While it is far from offering 'plug-and-play' ease of constructing incremental dialogue systems, we hope it will prove useful for other researchers insofar as it offers solutions to the more low-level problems that often are not one's main focus, but which need solving anyways before more interesting things can be done. We look forward to what these interesting things may be that others will build.

Acknowledgments

Most of the work decribed in this paper was funded by a grant from DFG in the Emmy Noether Programme.

References

G.S. Aist, J. Allen, E. Campana, L. Galescu, C.A. Gomez Gallo, S. Stoness, M. Swift, and M Tanenhaus. 2006. Software architectures for incremental understanding of human speech. In *Proceedings of the International Conference on Spoken Language Processing (ICSLP)*, Pittsburgh, PA, USA, September.

Timo Baumann, Michaela Atterer, and David Schlangen. 2009. Assessing and improving the performance of speech recognition for incremental systems. In *Proceedings of the North American Chapter of the Association for Computational Linguistics - Human Language Technologies (NAACL HLT) 2009 Conference*, Boulder, Colorado, USA, May.

Timo Baumann, Okko Buß, and David Schlangen. 2010. InproTK in action: Open-source software for building german-speaking incremental spoken dialogue systems. In *Proceedings of ESSV 2010*, Berlin, Germany.

Timo Baumann, Okko Buß, and David Schlangen. 2011. Evaluation and optimization of incremental processors. *Dialogue and Discourse*, 2(1):113–141.

Okko Buß, Timo Baumann, and David Schlangen. 2010. Collaborating on utterances with a spoken dialogue system using an isu-based approach to incremental dialogue management. In *Proceedings of the SIGdial 2010 Conference*, pages 233–236, Tokyo, Japan, September.

Adam Cheyer and David Martin. 2001. The open agent architecture. *Journal of Autonomous Agents and Multi-Agent Systems*, 4(1):143–148, March. OAA.

Ann Copestake. 2006. Robust minimal recursion semantics. Technical report, Cambridge Computer Lab. Unpublished draft.

Silvan Heintze, Timo Baumann, and David Schlangen. 2010. Comparing local and sequential models for statistical incremental natural language understanding. In *Proceedings of the SIGdial 2010 Conference*, pages 9–16, Tokyo, Japan, September.

Andreas Peldszus, Okko Buß, Timo Baumann, and David Schlangen. 2012. Joint satisfaction of syntactic and pragmatic constraints improves incremental spoken language understanding. In *Proceedings of the Conference of the European Association for Computational Linguistics (EACL 2012)*, Avignon, France, April.

Brian Roark. 2001. *Robust Probabilistic Predictive Syntactic Processing: Motivations, Models, and Applications*. Ph.D. thesis, Department of Cognitive and Linguistic Sciences, Brown University.

David Schlangen and Gabriel Skantze. 2009. A general, abstract model of incremental dialogue processing. In *Proceedings of the 12th Conference of the European Chapter of the Association for Computational Linguistics (EACL 2009)*, pages 710–718, Athens, Greece, March.

David Schlangen and Gabriel Skantze. 2011. A general, abstract model of incremental dialogue processing. *Dialogue and Discourse*, 2(1):83–111.

David Schlangen, Timo Baumann, and Michaela Atterer. 2009. Incremental reference resolution: The task, metrics for evaluation, and a bayesian filtering model that is sensitive to disfluencies. In *Proceedings of SIGdial 2009, the 10th Annual SIGDIAL Meeting on Discourse and Dialogue*, London, UK, September.

Gabriel Skantze and Anna Hjalmarsson. 2010. Towards incremental speech generation in dialogue systems. In *Proceedings of the SIGdial 2010 Conference*, pages 1–8, Tokyo, Japan, September.

Gabriel Skantze and David Schlangen. 2009. Incremental dialogue processing in a micro-domain. In *Proceedings of the 12th Conference of the European Chapter of the Association for Computational Linguistics (EACL 2009)*, pages 745–753, Athens, Greece, March.

Titus von der Malsburg, Timo Baumann, and David Schlangen. 2009. Telida: A package for manipulation and visualisation of timed linguistic data. In *Proceedings of the Poster Session at SIGdial 2009, the 10th Annual SIGDIAL Meeting on Discourse and Dialogue*, London, UK, September.

Willie Walker, Paul Lamere, Philip Kwok, Bhiksha Raj, Rita Singh, Evandro Gouvea, Peter Wolf, and Joe Woelfel. 2004. Sphinx-4: A flexible open source framework for speech recognition. Technical Report SMLI TR2004-0811, Sun Microsystems Inc.

A Simulation-based Framework for Spoken Language Understanding and Action Selection in Situated Interaction

David Cohen
Carnegie Mellon University
Nasa Research Park
Moffett Field, CA
david.cohen@sv.cmu.edu

Ian Lane
Carnegie Mellon University
Nasa Research Park
Moffett Field, CA
lane@cs.cmu.edu

Abstract

This paper introduces a simulation-based framework for performing action selection and understanding for interactive agents. By simulating the objects and actions relevant to an interaction, an agent can semantically ground natural language and interact considerately and on its own initiative in situated environments. The framework proposed in this paper leverages models of the environment, user and system to predict possible future world states via simulation. It leverages understanding of spoken language and multimodal input to estimate the state of the ongoing interaction and select actions based on the utility of future outcomes in the simulated world. In this paper we introduce this framework and demonstrate its effectiveness for in-car navigation.

1 Introduction

Speech and multimodal interactive systems have many challenges to overcome before they can effectively interact with users in the real world. These challenges include semantically grounding vague and ambiguous natural language utterances, understanding the user's knowledge and capabilities, and acting on their own initiative to plan and take appropriate actions in complex environments. To overcome these challenges, interactive agents require more than just models of the environment, user goals, and attention, they need the ability to infer the consequences of both their and the users' actions – a capability which simulation provides.

For each given task, an agent must plan the best way to carry it out. In many cases, a simple set of context-dependent behavior templates will not be sufficient. For example, if an in-car navigation assistant is trying to direct a driver to his destination, it should probably not give directions within the driver's own neighborhood, with which he is already familiar. However, it should inform the driver if there is road construction in the area of which he/she is unaware. Alternatively, if the driver is having an important conversation and the cost of the detour is outweighed by the cost of interrupting the conversation, perhaps the system should remain quiet. Understanding all the contexts that affect interaction is difficult and defining a set of heuristics to choose the appropriate behavior will quickly become unmanageable. An agent in the real world will be faced with complicated situations that will require planning and an understanding of the effects its actions will have.

To capture the full context necessary to perform understanding and planning in situated interaction, this paper argues for a unified model of the environment, the user's knowledge, attention and goals, and the simulated consequences of different courses of action.

2 Related Work

Early work in deep natural language understanding (Schank and Abelson, 1977; Wilensky, 1983) formed cognitive theories and developed software to reinforce the idea that understanding an agent's words requires an understanding of that agent's plans, goals, and planning mechanisms. Other work (Allen and Perrault, 1980) focused on identifying these plans and goals from the partial information available; interpreting speech acts as primitive actions in a STRIPS planner (Fikes and Nilsson, 1971), and using heuristics to determine an agent's plan based on their speech acts. Traum (1994) adopted a similar definition of speech acts, and developed a computational theory of grounding whereby multiple agents come to understand each other's plans and meaning.

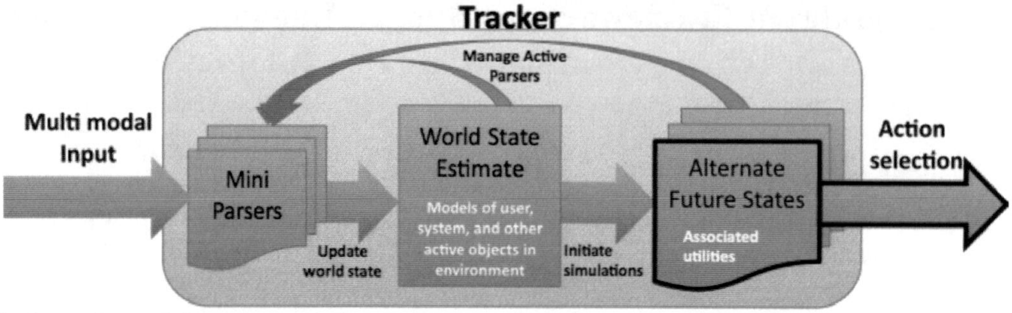

Figure 1: Overview of the proposed simulation-based understanding and action selection framework.

Previous work on considerate mixed-initiative systems has placed an emphasis on modeling the user's mental state, particularly attention and cognitive loading. Horvitz et al. (2003) treat attention as critical to reasoning about the value of taking action and potentially disrupting users. Multiple modalities such as speech and gesture recognition, as well as mouse and keyboard behavior all contribute to their models of attention. Their work also stressed the importance of attention cues in effective collaborative communication. Other work from the same author (Horvitz, 1999) probabilistically tracked a belief in the user's goal based on attentional cues, specifically trying to determine if a behavior from the system was desired. This work all reinforces the idea that close attention to the user's mental state must be paid to act considerately with mixed initiative, but never attempts to endow a system with the ability to reason about the consequences of its actions.

There are several existing paradigms for spoken dialogue systems. RavenClaw (Bohus and Rudnicky, 2009) uses a human-engineered task tree to guide the logic of an interaction, which allows for well-understood behavior, but does not permit the flexibility of planning needed for complex, dynamic interaction. The collaborative agent framework, COLLAGEN (Rich and Sidner, 1996), specifies the data structures for recipes and attention models based off the SharedPlan collaborative discourse framework. The framework proposed by Allen and et al. (2002) is built on a collaborative discourse framework similar to SharedPlan, and is similar to our work in its situation theoretic world model and focus on user goal and plan modeling. However, to the best of our knowledge, these frameworks have never been successfully applied to a situated agent in a dynamic environment with many interacting objects and a wealth of multi-modal input as is available within an in-car assistant environment. It is in these situations that we believe our framework will demonstrate its applicability compared to prior approaches.

3 A Simulation-based Framework for Understanding Situated Interaction[1]

In this paper, we propose a framework in which an interactive agent leverages a model of the ongoing situated interaction and simulations of possible future scenarios to perform understanding and decision-making (Figure 1). The model supports complex inference about natural language as well as other modalities of input, and provides a suitable environment for the system to evaluate possible courses of action. As an example, we evaluated the effectiveness of this framework for planning and interacting in an in-car navigation assistant.

Simulated Interaction and Environment

The system models its environment in terms of an object-oriented probabilistic model that allows for multiple simultaneous actions. It is assumed that the model is an incomplete view of the world, and there are objects that the model is unaware of. Included in this model is the set of primitive actions all the objects in the world can take, defined by their pre-conditions and post-conditions. Through simulation, the system can project the current world state forward in time in an attempt to predict possible futures. Within each simulated scenario, the system, user, and any number of other actors will interact. At each time step, every object selects a primitive action, which is applied to the world if its pre-conditions have been met.

[1] An initial version of the simulator used in the work can be download from: http://speech.sv.cmu.edu/SimInteraction

Programs for Modeling High-Level Actions

In order to make inferences about the long-term behavior of objects in the simulator, plans and high-level actions need a representation within the simulator. To do this, programs are defined for several realistic behaviors for each actor. These programs are a specific form of options (Sutton et al., 1999), which in the context of a Markov Decision Process are closed-loop policies for choosing action over an extended period of time.

In the current implementation, programs are finite state machines, which are resumed at each time interval, changing state based on the actor's internal state until a primitive action is selected.

Modeling User Knowledge and Awareness

An actor carrying out a program will choose a different sequence of actions depending on their internal mental state. That is why the world model must contain this information to make accurate predictions. In particular, a user's knowledge and attention play critical roles in their decision-making, and thus must be modeled.

Tracking and Parsing

The tracker maintains the current world model including the set of objects that are relevant for simulation and estimated distributions over uncertain variables such as the user's mental state and the programs being run by all relevant objects. The tracker is responsible for initiating simulations to project the situation model into the future. The tracker also manages and interfaces to a set of mini-parsers which interpret input across multiple modalities in various ways.

In the proposed framework, the tracker also uses information from the parsers to add new objects to the world model, and modify the parameters of the objects already in the model. Additional parsers can be spawned based on simulation results. For example, if a simulated scenario predicts the car running out of gas, the tracker might spawn a new parser to interpret the driver's awareness of their gas level based on gaze.

Utility Estimation and Action Selection

The desirability of every simulated scenario is determined by a utility score, defined by the system designer to maximize the system's usefulness. The system includes itself and its own possible programs in each simulation it runs, and picks the program that gives the best expected utility.

Table 1: Description of three evaluation tasks.

TaskID	Task Description
1	Destination is a business in downtown area, mostly a straight path as a warm-up task.
2	Destination is a residence in Palo Alto, insufficient gas to get to destination.
3	Destination is a residence in Mountain View, retrace much of the path from Task 2.

Table 2: Average number of system turns for baseline and the proposed system. System turns include questions, notifications, and instructions.

TaskID	Novice	Intermediate	Expert
1	7.0	7.0	3.0
2	13.0	15.8	9.0
3	12.0	12.8	9.0

4 Demonstration Example

We demonstrate the effectiveness of the proposed framework for an in-car navigation assistant. We tested this demonstration with ten test subjects each navigating through three the tasks listed in Table 1. The subjects navigated through Mountain View and Palo Alto, California in Google Earth™ while a supervisor observed their progress, entered it into the system and relayed messages between the subject and system. Some subjects had been in the area only a few times and some were current residents of Mountain View and neighboring cities. Based off the subjects' initial self-assessment, the system was given one of three different starting familiarity map estimates - novice, medium, and expert. These initial estimates reflected our intuitive assessment of the likelihood that a driver would know major streets and neighborhoods.

For users with different levels of familiarity we counted the number of system turns, which include questions, notifications, and instructions required to complete the task. These counts are shown in Table 2 show a decrease in the number of system turns across all tasks for users who were more familiar with the area. This is a direct result of the system's ability to direct these users to waypoints they were familiar with along the route, saving unnecessary directions. Example interactions obtained from the experiments are shown in Figure 1.

Novice	Intermediate	Expert
	Task 1	
S: "Go south on Moffett Blvd." ...	S: "Do you know how to get to Castro St. from here?" D: "Yes." S: "Go there." ...	S: "Go to Castro St." ...
	Task 2	
S: "You don't have enough gas for this trip." S: "Go south on Moffett Blvd." S: "Continue straight on Moffett Blvd." ...	S: "You don't have enough gas for this trip" S: "Do you know how to get to Shoreline and Central from here?" D: "Yes." S: "Go there." ...	S: "You don't have enough gas for this trip" S: "Go to Shoreline and Central." ...
	Task 3	
S: "Do you know how to get to Moffett and Middlefield from here?" D: "No." S: "Turn left onto Middlefield." ...	S: "Do you know how to get to Moffett and Middlefield from here?" D: "No." S: "Turn Left onto Middlefield." ...	S: "Do you know how to get to Moffett and Leong from here?" D: "I'm not sure." S: "Do you know how to get to Moffett and Middlefield from here?" D: "Yes." S: "Go there." ...

Figure 2: Sample interactions from subjects with different starting familiarity estimates.

5 Conclusions

This paper introduces a simulation-based framework for performing action selection and understanding in an interactive agent. The framework uses a simulator to predict possible future world states incorporating and updating models of the environment, user and system based on observed input. Understanding of spoken language and multimodal input is performed leveraging the past, current and future world states in the simulator. Action selection is performed based on the utility of future world states and the expected user goal. In this paper we introduce this framework and demonstrate its effectiveness for in-car navigation.

References

James Allen, Nate Blaylock, George Ferguson 2002. A Problem Solving Model for Collaborative Agents. Proc. AAMAS.

James F. Allen and C. Raymond Perrault. 1980. Analyzing Intention in Utterances. Artificial Intelligence.

Dan Bohus and Eric Horvitz. 2011. Multiparty Turn Taking in Situated Dialog: Study, Lessons, Directions Proc. SIGdial.

Dan Bohus and Alexander I. Rudnicky. 2009. The RavenClaw Dialog Management Framework: Architecture and Systems. Computer Speech and Language.

Richard E. Fikes and Nils J. Nilsson 1971. STRIPS: A New Approach to the Application of Theorem Proving to Problem Solving. IJCAI.

Eric Horvitz. 1999. Principles of Mixed-Initiative User Interfaces Proc. SIGCHI.

Eric Horvitz, Carl Kadie, Tim Paek, David Hovel. 2003. Models of Attention in Computing and Communication: From Principles to Applications. Communications of ACM.

Charles Rich and Candace L. Sidner 1996. COLLAGEN: When Agents Collaborate with People. Mitsubishi Electric Research Laboratories Inc.

Roger Schank and Robert Abelson. 1977. Scripts Plans Goals and Understanding: an Inquiry into Human Knowledge Structures. Lawrence Erlbaum Associates, Inc., Publishers.

Richard S. Sutton, Doina Precup, Satinder Singh. 1999. Between MDPs and semi-MDPs: A Framework for Temporal Abstraction in Reinforcement Learning. Artificial Intelligence.

David R. Traum. 1994. A Computational Theory of Grounding in Natural Language Conversation Ph.D. Thesis

Robert Wilensky. 1983. Planning and Understanding: A Computational Approach to Human Reasoning. The Addison-Wesley series in artificial intelligence.

Mining Search Query Logs for Spoken Language Understanding

Dilek Hakkani-Tür, Gokhan Tür, Asli Celikyilmaz
Microsoft, Mountain View, CA 94041, USA
dilek|gokhan.tur|asli@ieee.org

Abstract

In a spoken dialog system that can handle natural conversation between a human and a machine, spoken language understanding (SLU) is a crucial component aiming at capturing the key semantic components of utterances. Building a robust SLU system is a challenging task due to variability in the usage of language, need for labeled data, and requirements to expand to new domains (*movies, travel, finance*, etc.). In this paper, we survey recent research on bootstrapping or improving SLU systems by using information mined or extracted from web search query logs, which include (natural language) queries entered by users as well as the links (web sites) they click on. We focus on learning methods that help unveiling hidden information in search query logs via implicit crowd-sourcing.

1 Introduction

Building a robust spoken dialog system involves human language technologies to cooperate to answer natural language (NL) user requests. First user's speech is recognized using an automatic speech recognition (ASR) engine. Then a spoken language understanding (SLU) engine extracts their meaning to be sent to dialog manager for taking the appropriate system action.

Three key tasks of an SLU system are domain classification, intent determination and slot filling (Tur and Mori, 2011). While the state-of-the-art SLU systems rely on data-driven methods, collecting and annotating naturally spoken utterances to train the required statistical models is often costly and time-consuming, representing a significant barrier to deployment. However, previous work shows that it may be possible to alleviate this hurdle by leveraging the abundance of implicitly labeled web search queries in search engines. Large-scale engines, e.g., Bing or Google, log more than 100M queries every day. Each logged query has an associated set of URLs that were clicked after the users entered the query. This information can be valuable for building more robust SLU components, therefore, provide (noisy) supervision in training SLU models. Take domain detection problem: Two users who enter different queries but click on the same URL (www.hotels.com) would probably be searching for concepts in the same domain ("hotels" in this case).

The use of click information obtained through massive search query click logs has been the focus of previous research. Specifically, query logs have been used for building more robust web search and better information retrieval (Pantel and Fuxman, 2011; Li et al., 2008), improve personalization experience and understand social networking behaviors (Wang et al., 2011), etc. The use of query logs in spoken dialog research is fairly new. In this paper, we will survey the recent research on utilizing the search query logs to obtain more accurate and robust spoken dialog systems, focusing on the SLU. Later in the discussion section, we will discuss the implimications on the dialog models.

The paper is organized as follows: In § 2, we briefly describe query click logs. We then summarize recent research papers to give a snapshot of how user search queries are being used in § 3, and how information from click-through graphs (queries and

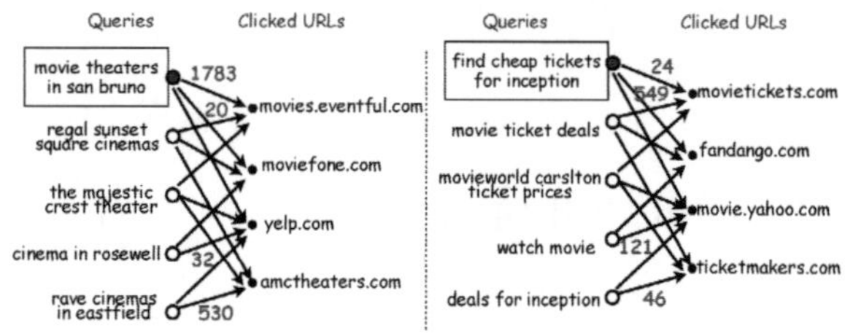

Figure 1: A sample query click graph. The squared queries are samples from training data which are natural language utterances. Edges include click frequencies from query to link.

clicked links) are exploited to boost the SLU performance. Lastly, we discuss possible future directions.

2 What are Query Click Logs (QCL)?

QCL are logs of unstructured text including both the users queries sent to a search engine and the links that the users clicked on from the list of sites returned by that search engine. A common representation of such data is a bi-partite query-click graph as shown in (Fig 1), where one set of nodes represents queries, and the other set of nodes represents URLs, and an edge is placed between two nodes representing a query q and a URL u, if at least one user who typed the q clicked on u.

Traditionally, the edge of the click graph is weighted based on the raw click frequency (number of clicks) from a query to a URL. Some of the challenges in extracting useful information from QCL is that the feature space is high dimensional (there are thousands of url clicks linked to many queries), and there are millions of queries logged daily.

3 Exploiting NL Search Queries for SLU

Previous work on web search has benefited from the use of query click logs for improving query intent classification. Li *et al.* use query click logs to determine the domain of a query (typically keyword search queries), and then infer the class memberships of unlabeled queries from those of the labeled search queries using the URLs the users clicked (Li et al., 2009; Li et al., 2008). QCL have been used to extract named-entities to improve web search and ad publishing experience (Hillard and Leggetter, 2010) using (un)supervised learning methods on keyword based search queries. Different from previous research, in this paper we focus on recent research that utilize NL search queries to boost the performance of SLU components, i.e., domain detection, intent determination, and slot filling.

In (Hakkani-Tur et al., 2011a), they use the search query logs for *domain classification* by integrating noisy supervision into the semi-supervised label propagation algorithm, and sample high-quality query click data. Specifically, they extract a set of queries, whose users clicked on the URLs that are related to their target domain categories. Then they mine query click logs to get all instances of these search queries and the set of links that were clicked on by search engine users who entered the same query. They compare two semi-supervised learning methods, self-training and label propagation, to exploit the domain information obtained form the URLs user have clicked on. The analysis indicate that query sampling through semi-supervised learning enables extracting NL queries for use in domain detection. They also argue that using raw queries with and without the noisy labels in semi-supervised learning reduces domain detection error rate by 20% relative to supervised learning which uses only the manually labeled examples.

The search queries found in click logs and the NL spoken utterances are different in the sense that the search queries are usually short and keyword based compared to NL utterances that are longer and are usually grammatical sentences (see Fig. 1). Hence, in (Hakkani-Tur et al., 2012), they choose a statistical machine translation (SMT) approach to search query mining for SLU as sketched in Fig. 2. The assumption is that, users typically have conceptual intents underlying their requests when they interact with web search engine or use a virtual assistance system with built in SLU engine, e.g., "*avatar awards*" versus "*which awards did the movie avatar win?*". They translate NL queries into search queries and mine similar search queries in QCL. They also exploit QCL for bootstrapping domain detection models, using only the NL queries hitting to seed domain indicator URLs (Hakkani-Tur et al., 2011c). Specifically, if one needs to detect a domain detector for the hotels domain, the queries hitting hotels.com, or tripadvisor.com, may be used to mine.

Query click logs have been explored for *slot filling* models as well. The slot filling models of SLU

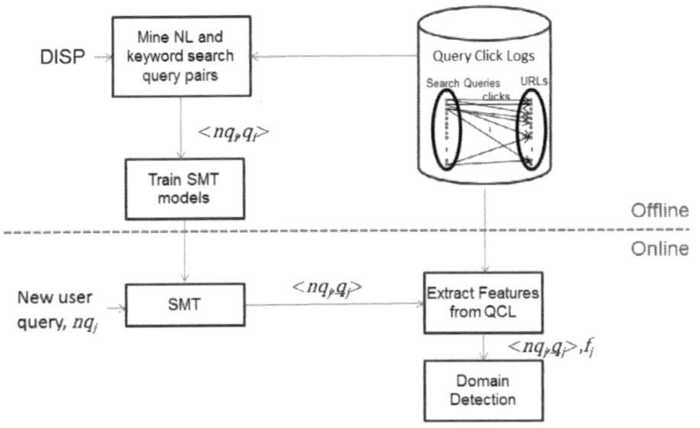

Figure 2: Using natural language to query language translation for mining query click logs.

aim to capture semantic components given the domain and a common way is to use gazetteer features (dictionaries specific to domain such as *movie-name* or *actors* in movie domain). In (Hillard et al., 2011), they propose to mine and weight gazetteer entries using query click logs. The gazetteer entries are scored using a function of posterior probabilities for that entry hitting a URL (compared to others URLs) and for that URL being related to the target domain. In such a schema the movie name "*gone with the wind*" gets higher score than the movie "*up*".

In (Tur et al., 2011), an unsupervised approach is presented to implicitly annotate the training data using the QCL. Being unsupervised, this method automatically populates gazetteers as opposed to manually crafted gazetteers. Specifically they use an abundant set of web search query logs with their click information (see Fig. 1). They start by detecting target URLs (such as `imdb.com/title` for the movie names). Then they obtain a list of entities and their target URLs (for example, www.imdb.com/title/tt047723 can be the target URL for the movie "*the count of monte carlo*". Then they extract all queries hitting those links if they include that entity. This method enables automatically obtaining annotated queries such as: "*review of* **the hand**" or "**mad men** *season one synopsis*" (***bold*** terms are automatically discovered entities.)

4 Mining Click Graph Features for SLU

In the previous section, we presented examples of recent research that use queries obtained from QCL to bootstrap and improve SLU models. Note that each query in QCL is linked to one or many web sites (links), which indicate a certain feature of the query (queries that the *hotels.com* linked are clicked after they are entered might indicate hotels domain). Such features extracted from QCL data (called click-through features) has been demonstrated to significantly improve the performance of ranking models for Web search applications (Gao et al., 2009), estimating relations between entities and web search queries (Pantel and Fuxman, 2011), etc.

In SLU research community, only recently the use of click-through features has shown to improve the performance of domain and intent of NL user utterances. In one study (Hakkani-Tur et al., 2011b), instead of mining more data to train a domain classifier with lexical features, they enrich their features using the click-through features with the intuition that the queries with similar click patterns should be semantically similar. They search all the NL utterances in the training data set amongst the search queries. Once they obtain search queries, they pull the list of clicked URLs and their frequencies for each query which represent the click features. To reduce the number of features, they extract only the base URLs (such as opentable.com or wikipedia.com), as is commonly done in the web search literature. T use the list of the 1000 most frequently clicked base URLs for extracting classification features (QCL features). For each input user utterance, x_j, they compute $P(URL_i|x_j)$, where $i = 1..1000$. They compute the click probability distribution distance between a query and the queries in a target domain, D_k, using the KL divergence:

$$KL_k = KL(P(URL_i|x_j)||P(URL_i|D_k)) \quad (1)$$

Thus, for a given domain D_k, the KL_k and the domain with the lowest KL divergence are used as additional features.

Although the click-through are demonstrated to be beneficial for SLU models, such benefits, however, are severely limited by the data sparseness problem, i.e., many queries and documents have no or very few clicks. The SLU models thus cannot rely strongly on click-through features. In (Celikyilmaz et al., 2011), the sparsity issue of representing the queries with click-through features are investigated. They represent each unlabeled query from QCL as a high dimensional sparse vector of click frequencies. Since the true dimensionality of a query is unknown (the number of clicks are infinitely many), they utilize an unbounded factor analysis approach and build an infinite dimensional latent factor analysis, namely the Indian Buffet Process (IBP) (Griffiths and Ghahramani, 2005), specifically to model the latent factor structure of the given set of queries. They implement a graph summarization algorithm to capture representative queries from a large set of unlabeled queries that are similar to a rather smaller set of labeled queries. They capture the latent factor structure of the labeled queries via IBP and reduce the dimensionality of the queries to manageable size and collect additional queries in this latent factor space. They use the new set of utterances boost the intent detection performance of SLU models.

5 Discussions and Future Directions

This paper surveyed previous research on the usage of the query click logs (the click through data) provide valuable statistics that can potentially improve performance of the SLU models. We presented several methods that has been used to extract information in the form of additional vocabulary, unlabeled utterances and hidden features to represent utterances. The current research is only the beginning, and most approaches such as query expansion, sentence compression, etc. can be easily adopted for dialog state update processes. Thus, the state-of-the art in NL understanding can be improved by:

- clustering of URLs as well as queries for extracting better features as well as to extend ontologies. The search community has access to vast amounts of search data that would benefit natural language processing research,
- mining multi-lingual data for transferring dialog systems from one language to others,
- mining information from search sessions, for example, users rephrasing of their own search queries for better results.

One issue that has been the topic of recent discussions is the accessibility of QCL data to researchers. Note that, QCL is not a crowd-source data that only large web search organizations like Google or Microsoft Bing can mine and exploit for NL understanding, but various other forms may be implemented by interested researchers by using a simple web service or a mobile app (such as AT&T SpeakIt or Dragon Go) or using a targeted search engine.

References

A. Celikyilmaz, D. Hakkani-Tur, and G. Tur. 2011. Leveraging web query logs to learn user intent via bayesian latent variable model. In *ICML'11 - WS on Combining Learning Strategies to Reduce Label Cost.*

J. Gao, J.-Y. Nie, W. Yuan, X. Li, and K. Deng. 2009. Smoothing clickthrough data for web search ranking. In *SIGIR'09.*

T. Griffiths and Z. Ghahramani. 2005. Infinite latent feature models and the indian buffet process. In *NIPS'05.*

D. Hakkani-Tur, G. Tur, and L. Heck. 2011a. Exploiting web search query click logs for utterance domain detection in spoken language understanding. In *ICASSP 2011.*

D. Hakkani-Tur, G. Tur, L. Heck, A. Celikyilmaz, A. Fidler, D. Hillard, R. Iyer, and S. Parthasarathy. 2011b. Employing web search query click logs for multi-domain spoken language understanding. In *ASRU'11.*

D. Hakkani-Tur, G. Tur, L. Heck, and E. Shriberg. 2011c. Bootstrapping domain detection using query click logs for new domains. In *Interspeech'11.*

D. Hakkani-Tur, G. Tur, R. Iyer, and L. Heck. 2012. Translating natural language utterances to search queries for slu domain detection using query click logs. In *ICASSP'12.*

D. Hillard and C. Leggetter. 2010. Clicked phrase document expansion for sponsored search ad retrieval. In *SIGIR'10.*

D. Hillard, A. Celikyilmaz, D. Hakkani-Tur, and G. Tur. 2011. Learning weighted entity lists from web click logs for slu. In *Interspeech'11.*

X. Li, Y.-Y. Wang, and A. Acero. 2008. Learning query intent from regularized click graphs. In *SIGIR08.*

X. Li, Y.-Y. Wang, and A. Acero. 2009. Extracting structured information from user queries with semi-supervised conditional random fields. In *ACM SIGIT'09.*

P. Pantel and A. Fuxman. 2011. Jigs and lures: Associating web queries with structured entities. In *ACL'11.*

G. Tur and R. De Mori, editors. 2011. *Spoken Language Understanding: Systems for Extracting Semantic Information from Speech.* John Wiley and Sons.

G. Tur, D. Hakkani-Tur, D. Hillard, and A. Celikyilmaz. 2011. Towards unsupervised spoken language understanding: Exploiting query click logs for slot filling. In *Interspeech'11.*

C. Wang, R. Raina, D. Fong, D. Zhou, J. Han, and G. Badros. 2011. Learning relevance from a heterogeneous social network and application in online targeting. In *SIGIR'11.*

HRItk: The Human-Robot Interaction ToolKit
Rapid Development of Speech-Centric Interactive Systems in ROS

Ian Lane[1], Vinay Prasad[1], Gaurav Sinha[1], Arlette Umuhoza[1], Shangyu Luo[1], Akshay Chandrashekaran[1] and Antoine Raux[2]
[1] Carnegie Mellon University, NASA Ames Research Park, Moffett Field, California, USA
[2] Honda Research Institute, Mountain View, California, USA
lane@cs.cmu.edu, araux@honda-ri.com

Abstract

Developing interactive robots is an extremely challenging task which requires a broad range of expertise across diverse disciplines, including, robotic planning, spoken language understanding, belief tracking and action management. While there has been a boom in recent years in the development of reusable components for robotic systems within common architectures, such as the Robot Operating System (ROS), little emphasis has been placed on developing components for Human-Robot-Interaction. In this paper we introduce HRItk (the Human-Robot-Interaction toolkit), a framework, consisting of messaging protocols, core-components, and development tools for rapidly building speech-centric interactive systems within the ROS environment. The proposed toolkit was specifically designed for extensibility, ease of use, and rapid development, allowing developers to quickly incorporate speech interaction into existing projects.

1 Introduction

Robots that operate along and with humans in settings such as a home or office are on the verge of becoming a natural part of our daily environment (Bohren et al., 2011, Rosenthal and Veloso 2010, Kanda et al., 2009, Srinivasa et al., 2009). To work cooperatively in these environments, however, they need the ability to interact with people, both known and unknown to them. Natural interaction through speech and gestures is a prime candidate for such interaction, however, the combination of communicative and physical actions, as well as the uncertainty inherent in audio and visual sensing make such systems extremely challenging to create.

Developing speech and gesture-based interactive robots requires a broad range of expertise, including, robotic planning, computer vision, acoustic processing, speech recognition, natural language understanding, belief tracking, as well as dialog management and action selection, among others. This complexity makes it difficult for all but very large research groups to develop complete systems. While there has been a boom in recent years in the development and sharing of reusable components, such as path planning, SLAM and object recognition, within common architectures, such as the Robot Operating System (ROS) (Quigley, 2009), little emphasis has been placed on the development of components for Human-Robot Interaction although despite the growing need for research in this area.

Prior work in Human-Robot Interaction has generally resulted in solutions for specific robotic platforms (Clodic et al., 2008) or standalone frameworks (Fong et al., 2006) that cannot be easily combined with standard architectures used by robotics researchers. Earlier work (Kanda et al., 2009, Fong et al., 2006) has demonstrated the possibilities of multimodal and multiparty interaction on robotic platforms, however, the tasks and interactions explored until now have been extremely limited, due to the complexity of infrastructure required to support such interactions and the expertise required to effectively implement and optimize individual components. To make significant progress, we believe that a common, easy to use, and easily extensible infrastructure, similar to that supported by ROS, is required for multi-modal human-robot interaction. Such a framework will allow researchers to rapidly develop initial speech and gesture-based interactive systems, enabling them to rapidly deploy systems, observe and collect interactions in the field and iteratively improve system components based on observed deficiencies. By using a common architecture and messaging framework, components and component models can easily be upgraded and extended by a community of researchers, while not affecting other components.

Towards this goal we have developed HRItk[1] (Human-Robot-Interaction toolkit), an infrastructure and set of components for developing speech-centric interactive systems within the ROS environment. The proposed toolkit provides the core components required for speech interaction, including, speech recognition, natural language understanding and belief tracking. Additionally it provides basic components for gesture recognition and gaze tracking.

[1] HRItk is available for download at: http://speech.sv.cmu.edu/HRItk

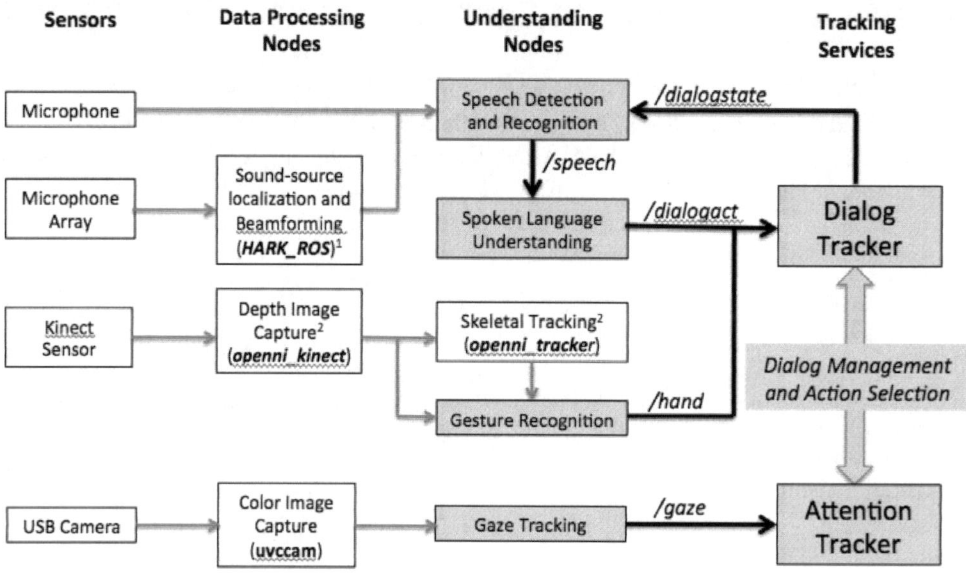

Figure 1: Overview of core understanding and tracking components within HRItk

2 Framework Overview

An overview of the core components in the toolkit are highlighted in Figure 1. We introduce two classes of components required for speech and multimodal interaction into the ROS framework, *understanding nodes* and *tracking services*. *Understanding nodes* are perceptual components that recognize and understand interaction events. Using input from sensors, intermediate processing nodes or other understanding components, these nodes generate hypotheses about current user input. *Tracking services* monitor the long term and continuous aspects of interaction, including user dialog goals and the user's focus of attention. These services are leveraged by components including Dialog Management and Action Selection to perform interaction. Additionally, these services provide context to *understanding nodes* enabling them to apply context-specific processing during the understanding phase.

2.1 Data Processing Nodes

The understanding components implemented in this work heavily leverage existing components developed in ROS (Quigley et al., 2009). These include the "*openni_kinect*" node, which processes depth-images from the Microsoft Kinect sensor, the "*openni_tracker*", which performs skeletal tracking, and "*uvccam*" node, which processes color images from external USB cameras. In the near future we also plan to support far-field speech recognition using the HARK_ROS toolkit (Nakadai et al., 2010).

2.2 Understanding Nodes

Understanding nodes recognize and understand events observed during interaction. As input they use either data obtained directly from sensors, preprocessed data from intermediate processing nodes or output from other understanding components. They either perform processing on explicit interaction events, such as speech or gesture input, or process continuous input such as joint position or gaze direction. The current *understanding nodes* implemented within HRItk are listed in Table 1 along with the ROS topics on which they publish.

Understanding nodes publish two forms of messages, "**state**" messages {`READY`, `START` and `STOP`}, indicating the state of the node and whether an interaction event has been detected, and "**hypothesis**" messages which enumerate the most likely observed events along with a likelihood measure for each. The specific structure of the "**hypothesis**" message is dependent on the event being observed.

2.3 State Tracking Services

In addition to understanding specific events such as utterances or gestures, an interactive system needs to track longer term and/or continuous aspects of interaction. Such aspects include user goals, which can span several utterances in a dialog, and the user's focus of attention (using, e.g., gaze and posture information). These can be defined as characterizing the *state* of the world (i.e. the user, the interaction, or the environment) at a given time, with possible reference to history.

Table 1: ROS nodes, Topics, Services and Messages implemented within HRItk

ROS Node	Topic / Service (*)	Description of Messages
Speech Detection and Recognition	speech/state	State identifying interaction event, each with a unique eventID
	speech/hypothesis speech/hypothesis/best speech/hypothesis/final	Partial and final hypotheses generated during speech recognition. Outputs include 1-best, N-best hypotheses and confusion networks. All output contains confidence or component model scores
	speech/context	Context indicating dialog-state, domain, task of current interaction
Natural Language Understanding	dialogact/hypothesis	Hypotheses of Concept/Value-pairs generated during NLU
	dialogact/context	Context indicating dialog-state, domain, task of current interaction
Gesture Recognition	hand/hypothesis	Hypothesis set of Gesture-Actions with confidence measure
	hand/context	Context indicating domain or task of current interaction
Gaze Tracking	gaze/hypothesis	Estimate of gaze direction
	hand/context	Context listing visually salient objects within users field of view
Dialog State Tracking	dialogstate/state	Receives an `UPDATED` message when the belief changes
	belief *	Belief over the concept set specified in the service request
	dialogstate/context	Context indicating system actions potentially affecting belief

In addition, states can be significantly larger objects than individual event understanding results, which could unnecessarily consume significant bandwidth if constantly broadcast. Therefore, state tracking modules use ROS *services* rather than topics to communicate their output to other modules. Any module can send a message to the tracking service containing a specific query and will receive in response the matching state or belief over states.

In order to allow components to react to changes in the state, each state-tracking module publishes an `UPDATED` message to its **state** topic whenever a new state is computed.

2.4 Component Implementations

Speech Detection and Recognition is performed using a ROS node developed around the Julius Speech Recognition Engine (Lee and Kawahara, 2009). We selected this engine for its compatibility with HARK (Nakadai et al, 2010), and its support of common model formats. A wrapper for Julius was implemented in C++ to support the ROS messaging architecture listed in Table 1. Partial hypotheses are output during decoding, and final hypotheses are provided in 1-best, N-best and Confusion Network formats. Context is supported via language model switching.

In order to develop a Speech Recognition component for a new task at minimum two component models are required, a pronunciation dictionary, and a language model (or recognition grammar). Within HRItk we provide the tools required to generate these models from a set of labeled example utterances. We describe the rapid model building procedure in Section 4.

Natural Language Understanding is implemented using Conditional Random Fields (Lafferty et al. 2001) similar to the approach described in (Cohn, 2007). For example, given the input utterance: "*Take this tray to the kitchen*" listed in Table 3, three concept/value pairs are extracted: `Action{Carry}, Object{tray}, Room{kitchen}`. Similar to the speech recognition component, the NLU component can be rapidly retrained using a set of tagged example sentences.

Gesture Recognition of simple hand positions is implemented using a Kinect depth sensor and previous work by Fujimura and Xu (2007) for palm/finger segmentation. Currently, the module publishes a hypothesis for the number of fingers raised by the user, though more complex gestures can be implemented based on this model.

Gaze Tracking is implemented using ASEF filters (Bolme et al., 2009) and geometric projection. Separate ASEF filters were training to locate the pupils of the left and right eye as well as their inner and outer corners. Filters were trained on hand-labeled images we collected in-house.

Dialog State Tracking is in charge of monitoring aspects of dialog that span multiple turns such as user goal. Our implementation is based on the Hound dialog belief tracking library developed at Honda Research Institute USA. Currently, our belief tracking model is Dynamic Probabilistic Ontology Trees (Raux and Ma 2011), which capture the hidden user goal in the form of a tree-shaped Bayesian Network. Each node in the Goal Network represents a concept that can appear in language and gesture understanding results. The structure of the network indicates (assumed) conditional independence between concepts. With each new input, the network is extended with evidence nodes according to the final understanding hypotheses and the system belief is estimated as the posterior probability of user goal nodes given the evidence so far.

A request to the dialog state tracking service takes the form of a set of concept names, to which the service responds with an m-best list of concept value assignments along with the joint posterior probability.

Examples.txt

<*Tagged example sentence*>	<***Action***>
`@Room{kitchen}`	**None**
`on the @Floor{fifth} floor`	**None**
`take this @Object{package} to @Room{room 123}`	**Carry**

Structure.txt

<*Node*>	<*Parent*>
Room	ROOT
Floor	Room
Object	Room

Figure 2: Training examples for robot navigation task

3 Rapid System Build Environment

The models required for the core interaction components in the system can be build from a single set of labeled examples ("*Examples.txt*"), along with a concept structure file ("*Structure.txt*") used by the Dialog State Tracker as shown in Figure 2. Running the automatic build procedure on these two files will generate 3 new models,

The data in the "Examples.txt" file is used to train the language model and pronunciation dictionary used by the Speech Detection and Understanding Node and the statistical CRF-parser applied in the Natural Language Understanding component. Given a set of labeled examples, the three models listed above are trained automatically without any intervention required from the user. Once a system has been deployed, speech input is logged, and can be transcribed and labeled with semantic concepts to improve the effectiveness of these component models.

As explained in section 3.5, our dialog state tracker organizes concepts in a tree structure. For a given domain, we specify that structure in a simple text file where each line contains a concept followed by the name of the parent concept or the keyword ROOT for the root of the tree. Based on this file and on the SLU data file, the resource building process generates the files required by the Hound belief tracker at runtime. This "off-the-shelf" structure assumes at each node a uniform conditional distribution of children values given the parent value. These distributions are stored in a human-readable text file and can thus be manually updated to more informative values.

Using the above tools, we have developed a sample using the proposed framework for robot navigation task. The entire system can be build from a single set of labeled examples as shown in Figure 3 used to train the language model and a component to perform actions on the SLU output.

4 Conclusions

In this paper we introduce HRItk (the Human-Robot-Interaction toolkit), a framework, consisting of messaging protocols, components, and development tools for rapidly building speech-centric interactive systems within the ROS environment. The proposed toolkit provides all the core components required for speech interaction, including, speech recognition, natural language understanding and belief tracking and initial implementations for gesture recognition and gaze tracking. The toolkit is specifically designed for extensibility, ease of use, and rapid development, allowing developers to quickly incorporate speech interaction into existing ROS projects.

References

Bohren J., Rusu R., Jones E., Marder-Eppstein E., Pantofaru C., Wise M., Mosenlechner L., Meeussen W., and Holzer S. 2011. *Towards autonomous robotic butlers: Lessons learned with the PR2*, Proc. ICRA 2011

Bolme, S., Draper, B., and Beveridge, J. 2009. *Average of Synthetic Exact Filters*, Proc. CVPR 2009.

Clodic, A., Cao, H., Alili, S., Montreuil, V., Alami, R. and-Chatila, R. *2008. Shary: A Supervision System Adapted to-Human-Robot Interaction.* In Proc. ISER 2008.

Cohn, T. 2007. *Scaling conditional random fields for natural language processing.* University of Melbourne.

Fong T., Kunz C., Hiatt L. and Bugajska M. 2006. *The Human-Robot Interaction Operating System.* Proc. HRI 2006.

Fujimura, K. and Xu, L. 2007. *Sign recognition using constrained optimization.* Proc. ACCV 2007.

Kanda, T., Shiomi M., Miyashita Z., Ishiguro H., and Hagita N. 2009. *An affective guide robot in a shopping mall.* In Proc. HRI 2009

Lafferty J., McCallum A., and Pereira F.. *Conditional random fields: Probabilistic models for segmenting and labeling sequence data.* In Intl. Conf. on Machine Learning, 2001.

Lee, A. and Kawahara, T. 2009. *Recent Development of Open-Source Speech Recognition Engine Julius.* Proc. Asia-Pacific Signal and Information Processing Association Annual Summit and Conference (APSIPA ASC), 2009.

Nakadai, K., Takahashi, T., Okuno, H.G., Nakajima, H., Hasegawa, Y., and Tsujino, H. 2010. *Design and Implementation of Robot Audition System "HARK".*

Quigley, M., Gerkey, B., Conley, K., Faust, J., Foote, T. Leibs, J., Berger, E., Wheeler, R. and Ng, A. 2009. *ROS: an open-source robot operating system.* Proc. Open-source Software Workshop, ICRA 2009.

Raux, A. and Ma, Y. 2011. *Efficient Probabilistic Tracking of User Goal and Dialog History for Spoken Dialog Systems.* Proc. Interspeech 2011.

Rosenthal S., Veloso M. 2010. *Using Symbiotic Relationships with Humans to Help Robots Overcome Limitations.* In Workshop for Collaborative Human/AI Control for Interactive Experiences 2010.

Srinivasa S., Ferguson D., Helfrich C., Berenson D., Collet A., Diankov R., Gallagher G., Hollinger G., Kuffner J., Vande-Weghe M. 2009. *Herb: A Home Exploring Robotic Butler.* Autonomous Robots, 2009

One Year of Contender: What Have We Learned about Assessing and Tuning Industrial Spoken Dialog Systems?

David Suendermann
SpeechCycle, New York, USA
david@suendermann.com

Roberto Pieraccini
ICSI, Berkeley, USA
roberto@icsi.berkeley.edu

Abstract

A lot. Since inception of Contender, a machine learning method tailored for computer-assisted decision making in industrial spoken dialog systems, it was rolled out in over 200 instances throughout our applications processing nearly 40 million calls. The net effect of this data-driven method is a significantly increased system performance gaining about 100,000 additional automated calls every month.

1 From the unwieldiness of data to the Contender process

Academic institutions involved in the research on spoken dialog systems often lack access to data for training, tuning, and testing their systems. This is simply because the majority of systems only live in laboratory environments and hardly get deployed to the live user[1]. The lack of data can result in systems not sufficiently tested, models trained on non-representative or artificial data, and systems of limited domains (usually restaurant or flight information).

On the other hand, in industrial settings, spoken dialog systems are often deployed to take over tasks of call center agents associated with potentially very large amounts of traffic. Here, we are speaking of applications which may process more than one million calls per week. Having applications log every action they take during the course of a call can provide developers with valuable data to tune and test the systems they maintain. As opposed to the academic world, often, there appears to be too much data to capture, permanently store, mine, and retrieve. Harddisks on application servers run full, log processing scripts demand too much computing capacity, database queues get stuck, queries slow down, and so on and so forth. Even if these billions and billions of log entries are eventually available for random access from a highly indexed database cluster, it is not clear what one should search for in an attempt to improve a dialog system's performance.

About a year and a half ago, we proposed a method we called Contender playing the role of a live experiment in a deployed spoken dialog system (Suendermann et al., 2010a). Conceptually, a Contender is an activity in a call flow which has an input transition and multiple output transitions (alternatives). When a call hits a Contender's input transition, a randomization is carried out to determine which alternative the call will continue with (see Figure 1). The Contender itself does not do anything else but performing the random decision during runtime. The different call flow activities and processes the individual alternatives get routed to make calls depend on the Contenders' decisions.

Say, one wants to find out which of ten possible time-out settings in an activity is optimal. This could be achieved by duplicating the activity in question ten times and setting each copy's time-out to a different value. Now, a Contender is placed whose ten alternatives get connected to the ten competing ac-

[1] One of the few exceptions to this rule is the Let's Go bus information system maintained at the Carnegie Mellon University in Pittsburgh (Raux et al., 2005).

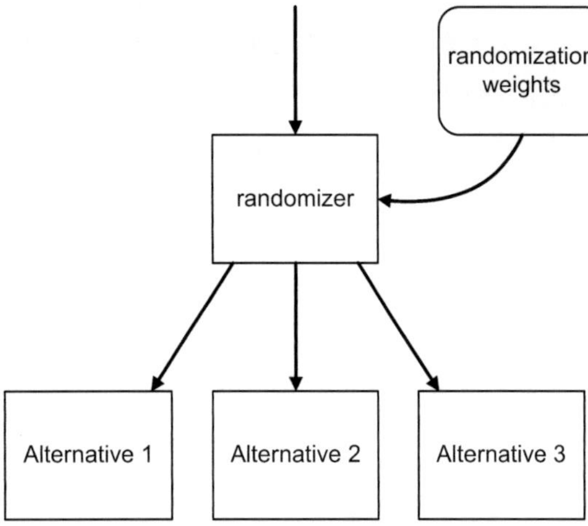

Figure 1: Contender with three alternatives.

tivities. Finally, the outbound transitions of the competing activities have to be bundled to make the rest of the application be independent of the Contender.

A Contender can be used for all sorts of experiments in dialog systems. For instance, if system designers are unsure about which of a number of prompts has more expressive power, they can implement all of them in the application and have the Contender decide at runtime which one to play. Or if it is unclear which actions to perform in which order, different strategies can be compared using a Contender. The same applies to certain parameter settings, error handling approaches, confirmation strategies, and so on. Every design aspect with one or more alternatives can be implemented by means of a Contender.

Once an application featuring Contenders starts taking live production traffic, an analysis has to be carried out, to determine which alternative results in the highest average performance. In doing so, it is crucial to implement some measure of statistical significance as, otherwise, conclusions may be misleading. If no statistical significance measure was in place, processing two calls in a two-way Contender, one routed to Alternative 1 and ending up automated and one routed to Alternative 2 ending up non-automated, could lead to the conclusion that Alternative 1's automation rate is 100% and Alternative 2's is 0. To avoid such potentially erroneous conclusions, we are using two-sample t-tests for Contenders with two alternatives and pairwise two-sample t-tests with probability normalization for more alternatives as measures of statistical significance. A more exact but computationally very expensive method was explained in (Suendermann et al., 2010a), but for the sake of performing statistical analysis with acceptable delays given the vast amount of data, we primarily use the former in production deployments.

If an alternative is found to statistically significantly outperform the other alternatives, it is deemed the winner, and it would be advisable routing most (if not all) calls to that alternative. While this hard reset maximizes performance induced by this Contender going forward, it sometimes takes quite a while before the required statistical significance is actually reached. Hence, in the time span before this hard reset, the Contender may perform suboptimally. Furthermore, even though statistical measures could indicate which alternative the likely winner is, this fact is potentially subject to change over time depending upon alterations in the caller population, the distribution of call reasons, or the application itself. For this reason, it is recommendable to keep exploring seemingly underperforming alternatives by routing a very small portion of calls to them.

The statistical model we discussed in (Suendermann et al., 2010a) presents a solution to the above listed issues. The model associates each alternative of a Contender with a weight controlling which percentage of traffic is routed down this alternative on average. As derived in (Suendermann et al., 2010a), the weight for an alternative is generated based on the probability that this alternative is the actual winner of the Contender given the available historic data. The weights are subject to regular updates computed by a statistical analysis engine that continuously analyzes the behavior of all Contenders in production deployment. In order to do so, the engine accesses the entirety of available application logs associating performance metrics, such as automation rate (the fraction of processed calls that satisfied the call reason) or average handling time (average call duration), with Contenders and their alternatives. This is relatively straightforward since the application can log call category (to tell whether a call was automated or not), call duration, the Contenders visited and the results of the randomization at each of the Contender. In Figure 2, a high-level diagram of the Contender process is shown.

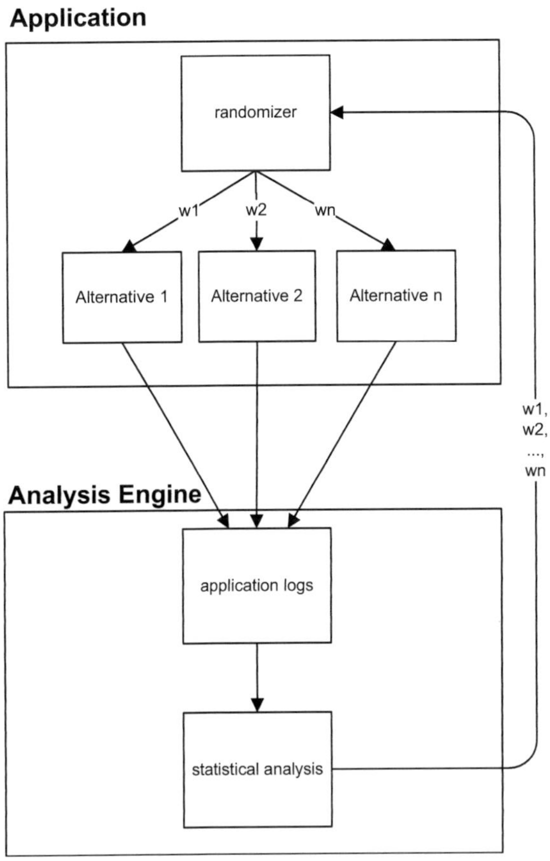

Figure 2: Contender process.

Since statistical analysis of Contenders involves data points of hundreds of thousands of calls, performance measurement needs to be based on automically derivable, i.e. objective, metrics. Popular objective metrics are automation rate, average handling time, "speech errors", retry rate, number of hang-ups or opt-outs (Suendermann et al., 2010c). There are also techniques correlating objective metrics to subjective ones in an attempt to predict user or caller experience, i.e., to evaluate interaction quality as perceived by the caller (Walker et al., 1997; Evanini et al., 2008; Möller et al., 2008). Despite the importance of making interactions as smooth and pleasant as possible, stakeholders of industrial systems often insist on using metrics directly tied to the savings generated by the deployed spoken dialog system. As we introduced in (Suendermann et al., 2010b), savings mainly depend on automation rate (A) and average handling time (T) and can be expressed by the reward

$$R = T_A A - T$$

where T_A is a trade-off factor that depends on average agent salary and hosting and telecommunication fees.

2 A snapshot of our last year's experiences

Shortly after setting the mathematical foundations of the Contender process and establishing the involved software and hardware pieces, the first Contenders were implemented in production applications. Under the close look of operations, quality assurance, engineering, speech science, as well as technical account management departments, the process underwent a number of refinement cycles. In the meantime, more and more Contenders were implemented into a variety of applications and released into production traffic. Until to date, 233 Contenders were released into production systems processing an total call volume of 39 million calls. Table 1 shows some statistics of a number of example Contenders per application. These statistics are drawn from spoken dialog systems for technical troubleshooting of cable services as discussed e.g. in (Acomb et al., 2007). Such applications assist callers fixing problems with their cable TV or Internet (such as no, slow, or intermittent connection, e-mail issues). In addition to the application and a short description of the Contender, the table shows three quantities:

- the number of calls processed by the Contender since its establishment (# calls),
- the reward difference between the highest- and lowest-performing alternative of a Contender ΔR (a high value indicates that the best-performing alternative is substantially better than the worst-performing one, that is, the Contender is very effective), and
- an estimate of the number of automated calls gained or saved per month by running the Contender ΔAt [mo^{-1}] (this value indicates the net effect of having all calls route through the best-performing alternative vs. the worst-performing one, that is, the upper bound of how many calls were gained or saved). This metric

Table 1: Statistics of example Contenders.

application	Contender	# calls	ΔAt [mo^{-1}]	ΔR
TV	problem capture	13,477,810	40,362	0.05
TV	cable box reboot order	4,322,428	28,975	0.11
TV	outage prediction	2,758,963	8,198	0.04
TV	on demand	485,300	8,123	0.17
TV	input source troubleshooting	1,162,445	3,487	0.05
TV	account lookup	9,627	3,201	0.02
Internet	troubleshooting paths I	275,248	5,568	0.02
Internet	troubleshooting paths II	1,389,489	3,530	0.01
Internet	computer monitor instruction	1,500,010	3,271	0.01
TV/Internet	opt in	6,865,929	31,764	0.05

is calculated by multiplying the observed difference in automation rate ΔA with the number of monthly calls hitting the Contender (t).

3 Conclusion

We have seen that the use of Contenders (a method to assess and tune arbitrary components of industrial spoken dialog systems) can be very beneficial in multiple respects. Applications can self-correct as soon as reliable data becomes available without additional manual analysis and intervention. Moreover, performance can increase substantially in applications implementing Contenders. Looking at only the 10 best-performing Contenders out of 233 running in our applications to-date, the number of automated calls increased by about 100,000 per month.

However, multiple Contenders that are active in the same call flow cannot always be regarded independent of each other. A routing decision made in Contender 1 earlier in the call can potentially have an impact on which decision is optimal in Contender 2 further down the call. In this respect, reward gains of Contenders installed in the same application are not necessarily additive. Not only can optimal decisions in a Contender depend on other Contenders but also on other runtime parameters such as time of the day, day of the week, geographic origin of the caller population, or the equipment used by the caller. Our current research focuses on evaluating these dependencies and accordingly optimize the way decisions are made in Contenders.

References

K. Acomb, J. Bloom, K. Dayanidhi, P. Hunter, P. Krogh, E. Levin, and R. Pieraccini. 2007. Technical Support Dialog Systems: Issues, Problems, and Solutions. In *Proc. of the HLT-NAACL*, Rochester, USA.

K. Evanini, P. Hunter, J. Liscombe, D. Suendermann, K. Dayanidhi, and R. Pieraccini:. 2008. Caller Experience: A Method for Evaluating Dialog Systems and Its Automatic Prediction. In *Proc. of the SLT*, Goa, India.

S. Möller, K. Engelbrecht, and R. Schleicher. 2008. Predicting the Quality and Usability of Spoken Dialogue Services. *Speech Communication*, 50(8-9).

A. Raux, B. Langner, D. Bohus, A. Black, and M. Eskenazi. 2005. Let's Go Public! Taking a Spoken Dialog System to the Real World. In *Proc. of the Interspeech*, Lisbon, Portugal.

D. Suendermann, J. Liscombe, and R. Pieraccini. 2010a. Contender. In *Proc. of the SLT*, Berkeley, USA.

D. Suendermann, J. Liscombe, and R. Pieraccini. 2010b. Minimally Invasive Surgery for Spoken Dialog Systems. In *Proc. of the Interspeech*, Makuhari, Japan.

D. Suendermann, J. Liscombe, R. Pieraccini, and K. Evanini. 2010c. 'How am I Doing?' A New Framework to Effectively Measure the Performance of Automated Customer Care Contact Centers. In A. Neustein, editor, *Advances in Speech Recognition: Mobile Environments, Call Centers and Clinics*. Springer, New York, USA.

M. Walker, D. Litman, C. Kamm, and A. Abella. 1997. PARADISE: A Framework for Evaluating Spoken Dialogue Agents. In *Proc. of the ACL*, Madrid, Spain.

Towards Quality-Adaptive Spoken Dialogue Management

Stefan Ultes, Alexander Schmitt, Wolfgang Minker
Dialogue Systems - Ulm University
Albert-Einstein-Allee 43
89081 Ulm, Germany
{stefan.ultes,alexander.schmitt,wolfgang.minker}@uni-ulm.de

Abstract

Information about the quality of a Spoken Dialogue System (SDS) is usually used only for comparing SDSs with each other or manually improving the dialogue strategy. This information, however, provides a means for inherently improving the dialogue performance by adapting the Dialogue Manager during the interaction accordingly. For a quality metric to be suitable, it must suffice certain conditions. Therefore, we address requirements for the quality metric and, additionally, present approaches for quality-adaptive dialogue management.

1 Introduction

For years, research has been focused on enabling Spoken Dialogue Systems (SDSs) to behave more adaptively to the user's expectations and needs. Möller et al. (2009) presented a taxonomy for quality of human-machine interaction, i.e., Quality of Service (QoS) and Quality of Experience (QoE). For QoE, several aspects are identified. They contribute to good user experience, e.g., interaction quality, usability and acceptability. These aspects can be combined to the term User Satisfaction (US), describing the degree by which the user is satisfied with the system's performance. The dialogue community has been investigating this aspect for years. Most prominently is the PARADISE framework by Walker et al. (2000) which maps objective performance metrics of an SDS to subjective user ratings.

Recent work mostly discusses how to evaluate Spoken Dialogue Systems. However, the issue of how this information can be useful for improving dialogue performance remains hardly addressed. Hence, we focus on exploring techniques for incorporating dialogue quality information into the Dialogue Manager (DM). This is accompanied by the problem of defining characteristics of a suitable dialogue quality metric.

In Section 2, we present related work both on measuring dialogue quality and on approaches for incorporating user state information into the DM. In Section 3, requirements for a quality metric are presented along with a suitable example. Section 4 presents our ongoing and future work on incorporating quality measures into dialogue strategies. Finally, Section 5 concludes this work.

2 Related Work

In recent years, several studies have been published on determining the qualitative performance of a SDS. Engelbrecht et al. (2009) predicted User Satisfaction on a five-point scale at any point within the dialogue using Hidden Markov Models (HMMs). Evaluation was based on labels the users applied themselves during a Wizard-of-Oz experiment. To guarantee for comparable conditions, the dialogue flow was controlled by predefined scenarios creating transcripts with equal length for each scenario.

Further work based on HMMs was presented by Higashinaka et al. (2010). The HMM was trained on US rated at each exchange. These exchange ratings were derived from ratings for the whole dialogue. The authors compare their approach with HMMs trained on manually annotated exchanges achieving a better performance for the latter.

In order to predict US, Hara et al. (2010) created n-gram models from dialogue acts (DA). Based on dialogues from real users interacting with a music retrieval system, overall ratings for the whole dialogue have been labeled on a five point scale after the interaction. An accuracy (i.e., rate of correctly predicted ratings) of 34% by a 3-gram model was the best performance which could be achieved.

Dealing with true User Satisfaction, Schmitt et al. presented their work about statistical classification methods for automatic recognition of US (Schmitt et al., 2011b). The data was collected in a lab study where the users themselves had to rate the conversation during the ongoing dialogue. Labels were applied on a scale from 1 to 5. Performing automatic classification using a Support Vector Machine (SVM), they achieved an Unweighted Average Recall (UAR) of 49.2 (i.e., average rate of correctly predicted ratings, compensated for unbalanced data).

An approach for affective dialogue modeling based on Partially Observable Markov Decision Processes (POMDPs) was presented by Bui et al. (2007). Adding stress to the dialogue state enables the dialogue manager to adapt to the user. To make belief-update tractable, the authors introduced Dynamic Decision Networks as means for reducing complexity.

Pittermann et al. (2007) presented another approach for adaptive dialogue management. The authors incorporated emotions by modeling the dialogue in a semi-stochastic way. Thus, an emotional dialogue model was created as a combination of a probabilistic emotional model and probabilistic dialogue model defining the current dialogue state.

3 Interaction Quality Metric

In order to enable the Dialogue Manager to be quality-adaptive, the quality metric must suffice certain criteria. In this Section, we identify the important issues and render the requirements for a suitable quality metric.

3.1 General Aspects

For adapting the dialogue strategy to the quality of the dialogue, the quality metric is required to implement certain characteristics. We identify the following items:

- exchange-level quality measurement,
- automatically derivable features,
- domain-independent features,
- consistent labeling process,
- reproducible labels and
- unbiased labels.

The performance of a Spoken Dialogue System may be evaluated either on the dialogue level or on the exchange level. As dialogue management is performed after each system-user exchange, dynamic adaption of the dialogue strategy to the dialogue performance requires exchange-level performance measures. Therefor, Dialogue-level approaches are of no use. Furthermore, previous presented methods for exchange-level quality measuring could not achieve satisfying accuracy in predicting dialogue quality (Engelbrecht et al., 2009; Higashinaka et al., 2010).

Features serving as input variables for a classification algorithm must be automatically derivable from the dialogue system modules. This is important because other features, e.g., manually annotated dialogue acts (Higashinaka et al., 2010; Hara et al., 2010), produce high costs and are also not available immediately during run-time in order to use them as additional input to the Dialogue Manager. Furthermore, for creating a *general* quality metric, features have to be domain-independent, i.e., not depending on the task domain of the dialogue system.

Another important issue is the consistency of the labels. Labels applied by the users themselves are subject to large fluctuations among the different users (Lindgaard and Dudek, 2003). As this results in inconsistent labels, which do not suffice for creating a generally valid quality model, ratings applied by expert raters yield more consistent labels. The experts are asked to estimate the user's satisfaction following previously established rating guidelines. Furthermore, expert labelers are also not prone to be influenced by certain aspects of the SDS, which are not of interest in this context, e.g., the character of the synthesized voice. Therefore, they create less biased labels.

3.2 Interaction Quality

As metric, which fulfills all previously addressed requirements, we present the Interaction Quality (IQ) metric, see also (2011a). Based on dialogues from the "Let's Go Bus Information System" of the Carnegie Mellon University in Pittsburgh (Raux et al., 2006), IQ is labeled on a five point scale. The labels are (from best (5) to worst (1)) "satisfied", "slightly unsatisfied", "unsatisfied", "very unsatisfied" and "extremely unsatisfied". They are applied by expert raters following rating guidelines, which have been established to allow consistent and reproducible ratings.

Additionally, domain-independent features used for IQ recognition have been derived from the dialogue system modules automatically for each exchange grouped on three levels: the *exchange level*, the *dialogue level*, and the *window level*. As parameters like ASRCONFIDENCE or UTTERANCE can directly be acquired from the dialogue modules they constitute the *exchange level*. Based on this, counts, sums, means, and frequencies of *exchange level* parameters from multiple exchanges are computed to constitute the *dialogue level* (all exchanges up to the current one) and the *window level* (the three previous exchanges).

A corpus containing the labeled data has been published recently (Schmitt et al., in press) containing 200 calls annotated by three expert labelers, resulting in a total of 4,885 labeled exchanges. Using statistical classification of IQ based on SVMs achieves an Unweighted Average Recall of 0.58 (Schmitt et al., 2011a).

4 Quality-Adaptive Spoken Dialogue Management

The goal of our work is to enable Dialogue Managers to directly adapt to information about the quality of the ongoing dialogue. We present two different approaches that outline our ongoing and future work.

4.1 Dialogue Design-Patterns for Quality Adaption

Rule-based Dialogue Managers are still state-of-the-art for commercial SDSs. It is hardly arguable that making the rules quality-dependent is a promising way for dialogue improvement. However, the number of possibilities for adapting the dialogue strategy to the dialogue quality is high. Based on the Speech-Cycle RPA Dialogue Manager, we are planning on identifying common dialogue situations in order to create design-patterns. These patterns can be applied as a general means of dealing with situations that arise by introducing quality-adaptiveness to the dialogue.

4.2 Statistical Quality-Adaptive Dialogue Management

For the incorporation of Interaction Quality into a statistical DM, two approaches have been found.

First, based on work on factored Partially Observable Markov Decision Processes by Williams and Young (2007) and similar to Bui et al. (2006), we presented our own approach for incorporating additional user state information (Ultes et al., 2011).

In the factored POMDP by Williams and Young (2007), the state of the underlying process is defined as $s = (u, g, h)$. To incorporate IQ, it is extended by adding the IQ-state s_{iq}, resulting in $s = (u, g, h, s_{iq})$.

Following the concept of user acts, we further introduce IQ-acts iq that describe the current quality predicted by the classification algorithm for the current exchange. Incorporating IQ acts into observation o results in the two-dimensional observation space

$$O = U \times IQ,$$

where U denotes the set of all user actions and IQ the set of all possible Interaction Quality values.

Second, for training an optimal policy for action selection in POMDPs, a reward function has to be defined. Common reward functions are task-oriented and based on task success and dialogue length. As an example, a considerable positive reward is given for reaching the task goal, a considerable negative reward for aborting the dialogue, and a small negative reward for each exchange in order to keep the dialogue short. Interaction Quality scores offer an interesting and promising way of defining a reward function, e.g., by rewarding improvements in IQ. By that, strategies that try to keep the quality at an overall high can be trained allowing for a better user experience.

5 Conclusion

For incorporating information about the dialogue quality into the Dialogue Manager, we identified characteristics of a quality metric defining necessary prerequisites for being used during dialogue management. Further, the Interaction Quality metric has been proposed as measure, which suffices all requirements. In addition, we presented concrete approaches of incorporating IQ into the DM outlining our ongoing and future work.

Acknowledgements

We would like to thank Maxine Eskenazi, Alan Black, Lori Levin, Rita Singh, Antoine Raux and Brian Langner from the Lets Go Lab at Carnegie Mellon University, Pittsburgh, for providing the Lets Go Sample Corpus. We would further like to thank Roberto Pieraccini and David Suendermann from SpeechCycle, Inc., New York, for providing the SpeechCycle RPA Dialogue Manager.

References

T. H. Bui, J. Zwiers, M. Poel, and A. Nijholt. 2006. Toward affective dialogue modeling using partially observable markov decision processes. In *Proceedings of workshop emotion and computing, 29th annual German conference on artificial intelligence*.

T. H. Bui, M. Poel, A. Nijholt, and J. Zwiers. 2007. A tractable ddn-pomdp approach to affective dialogue modeling for general probabilistic frame-based dialogue systems. In *Proceedings of the 5th IJCAI Workshop on Knowledge and Reasoning in Practical Dialogue Systems*, pages 34–37.

Klaus-Peter Engelbrecht, Florian Gödde, Felix Hartard, Hamed Ketabdar, and Sebastian Möller. 2009. Modeling user satisfaction with hidden markov model. In *SIGDIAL '09: Proceedings of the SIGDIAL 2009 Conference*, pages 170–177. ACL.

Sunao Hara, Norihide Kitaoka, and Kazuya Takeda. 2010. Estimation method of user satisfaction using n-gram-based dialog history model for spoken dialog system. In *Proceedings of the Seventh conference on International Language Resources and Evaluation (LREC'10)*, Valletta, Malta, may. ELRA.

Ryuichiro Higashinaka, Yasuhiro Minami, Kohji Dohsaka, and Toyomi Meguro. 2010. Modeling user satisfaction transitions in dialogues from overall ratings. In *Proceedings of the SIGDIAL 2010 Conference*, pages 18–27, Tokyo, Japan, September. Association for Computational Linguistics.

Gitte Lindgaard and Cathy Dudek. 2003. What is this evasive beast we call user satisfaction? *Interacting with Computers*, 15(3):429–452.

Sebastian Möller, Klaus-Peter Engelbrecht, C. Kühnel, I. Wechsung, and B. Weiss. 2009. A taxonomy of quality of service and quality of experience of multimodal human-machine interaction. In *Quality of Multimedia Experience, 2009. QoMEx 2009. International Workshop on*, pages 7–12, July.

Johannes Pittermann, A. Pittermann, Hong Meng, and W. Minker. 2007. Towards an emotion-sensitive spoken dialogue system - classification and dialogue modeling. In *Intelligent Environments, 2007. IE 07. 3rd IET International Conference on*, pages 239 –246, September.

Antoine Raux, Dan Bohus, Brian Langner, Alan W. Black, and Maxine Eskenazi. 2006. Doing research on a deployed spoken dialogue system: One year of lets go! experience. In *Proc. of the International Conference on Speech and Language Processing (ICSLP)*, September.

Alexander Schmitt, Benjamin Schatz, and Wolfgang Minker. 2011a. Modeling and predicting quality in spoken human-computer interaction. In *Proceedings of the SIGDIAL 2011 Conference*, Portland, Oregon, USA, June. Association for Computational Linguistics.

Alexander Schmitt, Benjamin Schatz, and Wolfgang Minker. 2011b. A statistical approach for estimating user satisfaction in spoken human-machine interaction. In *Proceedings of the IEEE Jordan Conference on Applied Electrical Engineering and Computing Technologies (AEECT)*, Amman, Jordan, December. IEEE.

Alexander Schmitt, Stefan Ultes, and Wolfgang Minker. in-press. A parameterized and annotated corpus of the cmu let's go bus information system. In *International Conference on Language Resources and Evaluation (LREC)*.

Stefan Ultes, Tobias Heinroth, Alexander Schmitt, and Wolfgang Minker. 2011. A theoretical framework for a user-centered spoken dialog manager. In *Proceedings of the Paralinguistic Information and its Integration in Spoken Dialogue Systems Workshop*, pages 241 – 246. Springer, September.

Marilyn Walker, Candace Kamm, and Diane Litman. 2000. Towards developing general models of usability with paradise. *Nat. Lang. Eng.*, 6(3-4):363–377.

Jason D. Williams and Steve J. Young. 2007. Partially observable markov decision processes for spoken dialog systems. *Computer Speech and Language*, (21):393–422.

Author Index